PAY THE PEOPLE!

PAY THE PEOPLE!

**Why Fair Pay Is Good for Business and
Great for America**

John Driscoll, Morris Pearl
& The Patriotic Millionaires

THE
NEW
PRESS

NEW YORK
LONDON

Requests for permission to reproduce selections from this book should be made through our website: https://thenewpress.com/contact.

Epigraph quote from Rick Wartzman, *Still Broke: Walmart's Remarkable Transformation and the Limits of Socially Conscious Capitalism* (New York: PublicAffairs, 2022), 170.

Published in the United States by The New Press, New York, 2024
Distributed by Two Rivers Distribution

ISBN 978-1-62097-882-5 (pb)
ISBN 978-1-62097-898-6 (ebook)

CIP data is available

The New Press publishes books that promote and enrich public discussion and understanding of the issues vital to our democracy and to a more equitable world. These books are made possible by the enthusiasm of our readers; the support of a committed group of donors, large and small; the collaboration of our many partners in the independent media and the not-for-profit sector; booksellers, who often hand-sell New Press books; librarians; and above all by our authors.

www.thenewpress.com

Book design by Bookbright Media
Composition by Dix Digital Prepress and Design
This book was set in Minion Pro

Printed in the United States of America

10 9 8 7 6 5 4 3 2 1

How am I going to sell my refrigerators if we don't give 'em wages to buy with?

—Charlie Wilson, president of General Electric, 1944

Contents

Introduction

Seventy-one percent of Americans think the economy is rigged against them. We have news for them: they are right. Over decades, politicians of both parties coddled the political donor class, screwed working people, and broke the social contract by passing laws that structured the economy in such a way that the wealth created by millions of working people was driven into the hands of a tiny number of very rich people. In 1973, the top 1 percent took home 9 percent of the income in the country.[1] In 2023, the top 1 percent took home 26.5 percent of the country's income.[2] One researcher estimates that since 1981, as much as $50 trillion has moved from the bottom 90 percent to the top 1 percent.[3] What happened in the United States is pretty simple. As Americans worked harder and the economy grew, working people stopped getting their fair share and the richest among us made out like bandits. They did it with the help of expensive lobbyists and enabling politicians, and they destabilized the entire country in the process.

The Patriotic Millionaires first came together in 2010 during the lame-duck session of Congress when it became clear that President Obama was going to cave to Republican demands to extend the George W. Bush tax cuts. Fifty-six Americans with annual incomes over $1 million signed a letter urging lawmakers to "put our country ahead of politics" and increase taxes on millionaires like them. We called ourselves the "Patriotic Millionaires" because, as one signer put it, "our country is way more important than my money." The organization now has a few hundred members in the United States and another handful in the United Kingdom. In the last three years, more than a thousand millionaires from across the globe have joined the call to tax the rich and reform our economic structure before it's too late.

The Patriotic Millionaires come from a range of backgrounds. Some grew up with nothing and built their fortunes, others inherited their wealth. There are some members you have likely heard of—George Zimmer, founder of the Men's Wearhouse, and filmmaker Abigail Disney (and granddaughter of Roy Disney)—plus many others you likely haven't. One member founded a company that prints plastic gift cards; another started a chain of grocery stores; another created some of the technology on the Mars rover. Several made their money in investment management, others in law. One member was a boatbuilder who married into money. When he saw the first tax return he filed after his marriage, he called his accountant to demand why, as a wealthy person, he was now paying half the tax rate he paid when he was sweating in the sun cold-molding wooden hulls.

What all these people have in common (aside from being very rich) is that they are deeply concerned about the future of this country. They also live here and work here and raise children and grandchildren here. They see what's going on and they want to help fix it. Not because they are charitable or kind, but because they recognize what a lot of other rich people can't seem to grasp: a society this unequal will not stand. In the game of economic Jenga, when enough blocks are taken from the bottom and the middle and loaded onto the top, eventually the whole thing will collapse. This will be bad for everyone, including rich people. As our board chair Morris Pearl (one of the authors of this book) often says, "I'm not any more altruistic than the next person; I'm just greedier for a different kind of country than a lot of other rich people."

The Patriotic Millionaires first came together over taxes. Then, in 2012, fast-food workers in New York City walked off the job to protest starvation pay, and the Fight for $15 was born. We saw that taxes were only half of the equation— the other half was wages. A great economy requires two things: a smart tax code and a solid wage floor. We need a tax code that prevents destabilizing levels of inequality by redirecting excessive accumulated wealth away from individuals and corporations and toward public invest- ment that benefits the entire citizenry, and a wage floor that is high enough and strong enough to hold up a large and prosperous middle class. In some ways, you could con- sider taxation as a way to *re*-distribute the proceeds of the economy, and wages as the easiest and most efficient way to *pre*-distribute the proceeds of the economy.

Right now, we have a tax code that values each dollar a rich person makes more than each dollar a working person makes. And we have a wage floor that is too low and too porous. Think of taxes and wages as the bookends of a strong economy. If structured right, they hold the entire society upright and together. And if one or both bookends aren't strong enough, it simply will not hold.

In 2021 we released *Tax the Rich! How Lies, Loopholes, and Lobbyists Make the Rich Even Richer*. That book provided a top-to-bottom explanation of exactly how the tax code rigs the economy in favor of the rich—and, more importantly, how to unrig it so that it works for the whole country. In this book, we turn to the other side of the equation: the wage floor, otherwise known as the minimum wage.

There's an old *Saturday Night Live* skit where Chevy Chase, playing President Gerald Ford, responds to an economic question in a presidential debate by saying, "It was my understanding there would be no math during the debates." That seems to be the problem with a lot of Washington lawmakers. They've forgotten that there *is* math in this debate. It's called the cost of living. And for most people, the math just doesn't add up. More than 40 percent of working people in America—over 50 million people—make less than the cost of living for a single person working in low-wage jobs, which include everything from retail clerks to home health aides to cooks. For most of them, especially those with kids, it's simply not enough to make ends meet.

When you really look at the math, you see that there is a simple solution to what ails the nation, and it can be summed up in three little words: pay the people. That's right, the single most efficient, effective (and obvious) way to stabilize the economic lives of working people—and the country—is to make sure that their jobs pay enough so they can meet their cost of living. It is time to reconnect the prosperity of American families to the success of American businesses. When businesses do well, all the people who work for those businesses should do well too—not just the ones in the C-suite. That begins by paying people something close to the actual cost of living. It's simple. If you can't afford to pay an employee something they can live on, you can't afford an employee. If you're making money while everyone who works for you struggles to survive, you aren't running a business, you're running a human exploitation scheme.

Consider this: from 1948 to 1973, productivity rose by 97 percent while hourly compensation rose by 91 percent.[4] During these years, workers received the benefit of increased productivity in the form of higher wages. After 1973, productivity continued to rise, but compensation no longer rose with it. From 1973 to 2014, productivity rose by 72.2 percent while hourly compensation rose only 9.2 percent. Essentially all the productivity gains made post-1973 accrued to the owners of companies rather than the workers themselves. Productivity and compensation became decoupled in the mid-1970s and have remained uncoupled since then. But why? Look no further than the declining value of the nation's minimum wage.

Stop for a minute here. Stomp your foot on the floor. Now stand up and jump up and down. Did the floor collapse? If so, we're terribly sorry, but that will teach you how important it is to have a solid floor underneath you. The wage floor is like that. The minimum wage—the wage floor—provides a foundation on which wages much further up rest. Would you rather have a floor with lots of holes in it, or a solid floor that you can jump up and down on? Ask yourself that question every time someone challenges the idea that a strong wage floor is essential to a strong middle class.

Today, there is not a single state in the country where the minimum wage is equal to the cost of living for a single person with no children. Not one. Put another way, there is nowhere in the country where a single person working full-time can support themselves on minimum wage. The "living wage gap," the difference between what it costs to live somewhere and the hourly minimum wage, is substantial and growing—ranging from $7.89 per hour in Maine to a whopping $16.04 per hour in Georgia. Twenty states with the biggest gaps follow the federal minimum wage of $7.25.[5]

This hasn't always been the case. In 1968, two things happened: McDonald's introduced the Big Mac, and the minimum wage reached its peak buying power. Minimum wage in that year was $1.60 per hour,[6] while a Big Mac went for 49¢.[7] In 1968, if you worked an hour at a minimum-wage job, you could buy 3.25 Big Macs. Today, if you work an hour at a minimum-wage job, you can only buy 1.5 Big Macs (and no fries!).[8]

The minimum wage has gone up a few times since 1968, but never enough to maintain its peak purchasing power. If the minimum wage had kept up with inflation since 1968, today it would be a little over $14.[9] A minimum wage at that level would push wages for everyone else up. So a person making $14 an hour now would likely make closer to

$20 an hour. That's a big difference. The level of the minimum wage will be even more important as automation and artificial intelligence continue to advance. We will be able to produce everything our society needs with fewer people. This could be a good thing—even a great thing for humanity—only if we ensure the remaining jobs pay enough to support the rest of the population.

What ails the country now has been ailing the country for a long time. It's not going to change unless we all work together to fix the economy so that regular people get a fair share of the pie. While we pledge allegiance to the red, white, and blue, let's also make sure we talk about the green: money.

The goal of the Patriotic Millionaires organization is to reform the nation's economy so that it naturally delivers the results we need for a stable, prosperous nation. The way the economy is currently structured guarantees that over time we will become more unequal, even more quickly. We are already at one-hundred-year-level highs of inequality. We broke the social contract and, in the process, broke the country. People are struggling daily just to meet their basic needs while Jeff Bezos is climbing into his personal rocket ship for a joyride in space.

The economy should not be judged on how many billionaires it can mint in a calendar year, but rather on whether or not it meets the needs of the people living in the country. In fact, one could argue that the more billionaires an economy produces, the less likely it is to be meeting the needs of everyone else. Prolonged and growing inequality, such as we are seeing right now, eventually causes a breakdown of civil society. If left unchecked, concentrated wealth will lead to a wholesale dismantling and eventual death of liberal democracy, human rights, and freedom. As Louis Brandeis said, "We may have democracy, or we may have wealth concentrated in the hands of a few, but we can't have both."

If we don't fix the economy, the United States of America will never have the chance to realize its full potential. Instead of the land of the free and the home of the brave, we are heading toward a land of the serf and the home of the totally exhausted. The nation is on the edge. The future is ours to decide and the decisions are easy ones. We can steer the country through this self-inflicted period of divisiveness and social unrest and into a stable, inspiring future, provided we do two things: tax the rich, and pay the people before it's too late.

The stakes are high, and the time is short. Let's get to it.

John Driscoll's Story

In 2014, I took over a troubled health care services company called CareCentrix, where entry-level employees made the federal minimum wage of $7.25 (about $15,000 a year for full time work). Revenue was down; turnover was up. It was my job to stop the hemorrhaging.

As the new CEO, I made sure that our employees could reach me directly to introduce themselves, share thoughts about the company, vent, identify problems, or suggest solutions. My inbox was soon flooded. And some of those emails were absolutely heartwrenching.

One was from a customer service representative, a single mother with two small children. She lost her apartment and her possessions in a fire and was "really sorry" to bother me—she must have repeated that three times in her short note—but she didn't have enough money to buy diapers. Could I possibly authorize an advance on her pay?

Another painful note came from a team member who was looking for help in paying the funeral expenses for a child who had just died.

The email that put me over the edge was from an employee— effective and well-liked by her team—who had fallen behind on bills and rent, lost her apartment, and was sleeping overnight in her car with her daughter.

This drove me crazy: how did we get to the point where full-time employees couldn't afford to put a roof over their heads, or had to beg for an advance on their paycheck to buy diapers? Something had to change. Our struggling company had to find a way to pay hundreds of employees more money.

CareCentrix was headquartered in the Stilts Building in downtown Hartford, Connecticut, when I joined. The building's name derives from an illusion created by its architectural design: the top floors look like they might topple over or collapse. At the time, the company felt like a good match for the building; I was replacing the previous CEO who was leaving as fast as I could show up. The chief medical officer quit the week before I started, and the company had been running an unsuccessful search to replace their chief financial officer for months. After a very pleasant lunch with me on a my first day, the chief operating officer quit. The company was, in short, a total mess.

Things hadn't always been so bad. CareCentrix was a high growth health care company that helped patients avoid unnecessary stays in hospitals and nursing homes, and also managed patients after being discharged. Over the prior three years before I joined, the company had more than tripled in size. We had entry-level jobs in all our offices, in departments like customer service and claims payment. We provided opportunities that helped new employees with high school degrees transition into professional pathways and development. If you joined CareCentrix in one of our entry-level jobs and performed well, you had the chance to build a promising career. We were so successful that state governors in Connecticut and Florida hailed our company as a model for creating jobs.

As a health care company focused on the service and support of vulnerable patients and their families, we relied on not only the skills of our teammates, but also on their passion and hearts. Almost no one enters the health care system by choice. Whether from an accident or a chronic illness, nearly everyone who needs health care starts from a position of personal vulnerability. Our health care system is infuriatingly complicated. When we hire a new employee, we ask that they not just do their jobs—executing tasks like answering a benefit question or paying a claim—but that they do so with care and compassion. It is what every person deserves, but does not always get, from the American health care system.

Yet, while we were asking so much from our employees, we were failing to extend that same level of kindness and care to them. Somewhere along the way, CareCentrix lost the essence of what powered its success in the first place—the people and teams working each day to help patients navigate the byzantine maze of the U.S. health care system. CareCentrix was floundering. Our margins were declining, and our revenue growth had stalled. As a private company, our investors expected us to grow revenue, cut costs and increase profits. In many companies, that means low wages and layoffs, but the more I learned about our business and our employees, the more determined I was to find a different playbook.

Like many companies large and small in the United States, all our entry-level employees started at the federal minimum wage: then, as now, just over $7.25 per hour. According to our human relations team, this was industry standard—what is often called "market." We had no shortage of people applying to start careers with us. In fact, we had far more applicants for our entry-level jobs than we had available slots. From the perspective of previous management and our recruiting department, if we were attracting more applicants than we had open positions for, then our wages must be fine.

Yet I was increasingly troubled by our turnover numbers. "Turnover" refers to employees who join a company but leave within a year. Recruiting and training new employees is an expensive process. In several entry-level areas, our turnover numbers were crazy high: 30 to 50 percent of our employees were leaving within a year.

Some of our executives and HR leaders suggested that we not worry too much about our turnover stats. They recommended that we simply ignore all of the employees that quit within the first three to six months. High turnover numbers are common in entry-level jobs, and my team suggested that we rethink recruiting instead. I understood that there is always room to recruit more carefully, but I wondered if our lean compensation policies could be the problem. Was it possible that we were hiring good employees who could not afford to keep their jobs?

Reading the emails from some of our teammates and listening to their life experiences gave me a real understanding of how badly we were failing the people who were a critical part of our business. What became crystal clear to me was that the legal definition of a "minimum" wage was well below the minimum amount that it actually costs to live, or even to functionally survive. There is no county in the United States where a single person can live on $15,000 a year. Maybe in some markets an individual could afford to live on the minimum wage—assuming they lived with other wage-makers, and nothing ever went wrong. Of course, this is unrealistic; some things do go wrong. Life never goes completely according to plan. Spouses leave. Young kids get sick. Parents die. Surprise bills show up. Yes, we were legally allowed to pay people a wage we knew they could not survive on. That didn't mean we should.

Was providing less than enough cash to live on really a "career path"? What kind of life did our teammates lead if they were consistently worried about paying for rent or food? We knew from talking to our team at all levels that some of them struggled to pay their bills. A few days prior to Thanksgiving one of our vice presidents noticed that our Tampa refrigerators were packed with turkey and vegetables. It turned out that one of our managers had bought cartloads of food for our employees who couldn't afford a turkey dinner for their families. How could we be proud of jobs that paid so little that some staffers couldn't afford a holiday meal?

About six months into my new job as CEO I started to dig into our compensation plans. Like many companies, we kept our entry-level jobs at the legal minimum wage, while we adjusted more senior jobs for inflation. Because the federal minimum wage hasn't been raised in years and because inflation goes up most years, if you joined us at an entry-level position, you would effectively be doing the same job for less money every year. The practical result of this structure was that many employees started at a lower salary each year while top earners marched consistently higher.

As I pored over requests for help from our employees, I weighed solutions. Could we pass the hat, raise money from our executives, and write checks to take care of some of our employees' bigger challenges? No, periodic charity would never fix the problems of our lowest-wage employees. We had to find a way to increase their pay permanently.

I thought hard and ultimately came up with a novel idea. My idea was this: What if we froze the wages of the senior team and invested their year-over-year inflation adjustment into raising the wages of our entry-level employees? The challenge was twofold: First, we needed to figure out what precisely constituted a livable wage. When we discussed this issue in 2014 there seemed to be a rough consensus that a $15 per hour wage rate was a reasonable aspirational goal to achieve. Fewer than half of our team members made $15 per hour. Second, we needed to understand how deep into our executive ranks we would have to go in freezing wages in order to raise our team members' base wages. We did not have to go very deep at all—fewer than twenty well-paid executives, as it turns out.

This might sound simple, but it wasn't a risk-free decision. At the time I proposed more than doubling the wages we paid, the company was in financial trouble. Some people thought we couldn't afford to pay more. I decided we couldn't afford not to pay more. The bet we made—successfully—relied on the enlightened self-interest of management and on the goodwill of our team. I believed that the only rational way we could expect great work from nearly half of the company was to make sure they didn't have to suffer to succeed.

Over the last few decades, executive salaries have skyrocketed. That has translated into accelerated wage growth for executives throughout American business. Our small company was no different. As such, by freezing the wages of fewer than twenty of our executives, we could dramatically raise the wages of almost five hundred people. Five hundred people who, incidentally, delivered the care we had built a company around.

We were not required to make this change, but it was the right thing to do. First, it made good business sense. If we aspired to position the company for long-term success, we needed lower turnover and a more stable team. All of us at the executive level aimed to turn CareCentrix into a high-performing company—doing that required commitment, compassion, and competence at all levels of our organization. How could we push our team members to work harder and smarter if some of them found it hard to survive on what we paid them? It was up to us, as executives, to show that we believed in them and would personally invest some of our salaries to balance and improve their wages.

I went to my senior managers, eighteen people in all, and said: "It makes no sense that we have over half of our workforce earning substantially less than $15 an hour. That's not enough to survive and succeed. Do you think it is reasonable that—starting with me—we freeze salary increases and merit increases for a year and invest that, plus some other cash, to bring them up to $15?" It doesn't take much sacrifice at the top to substantially increase the bottom. "Yes, we will be taking the risk that we'll have to earn more money as a company, but by doing this, we'll have more of our employees focused on helping us do that. Is that a good bet?"

We talked at the executive level about the day-to-day crises that some of our team members experienced. We knew many of our co-workers were struggling. The incremental year-over-year wage increase was important to some of our executives but nowhere near as critical as it was to those who were juggling with bills they could not pay.

Some of the conversations were long, and they weren't all pleasant, but in the end, not one person pushed back. Over the next ten years, we continued to invest in our employees: raising everyone's wages to track inflation, including each team member in our bonus programs, and ensuring affordable health care for every employee. Our investments in our people paid off and translated directly into greater success for our business. CareCentrix returned to growth, more than tripled in size and more than quadrupled in value, before we sold the company to Walgreens in 2022.

This Isn't About Morals, It's About Money

My decision to raise wages for workers at CareCentrix was absolutely influenced by my sense of morality. I wanted to do the right thing for the employees who relied on us. But it is not a remarkable insight to recognize that paying workers more helps them pay their bills. Every business leader knows, at least on some level, that paying struggling low-wage workers more would be the "right" thing for them to do. They're familiar with the argument that it's wrong to overpay themselves and shareholders and underpay workers. They've probably heard it many times over the course of their careers. And yet they keep doing it. Carecentrix would have kept doing it too, if I hadn't realized that it wasn't just the right thing to do for our employees, it was the right thing to do for the business.

That's the difference, and that's the case we want to prove in this book. The moral arguments clearly aren't sufficient. The incentive structure within the C-suite in most companies gives executives little reason to care about the "right" thing to do, and every reason to care about what is going to maximize quarterly profits and their stock price in the short term. Even executives who want to do better for their workers are often beholden to their shareholders and board, who demand that they be ruthless in their pursuit of short-term profits.

I believe capitalists are spoiling capitalism for all of us. I've seen first hand how corporations have done such a good job at driving costs and wages down that the bottom is falling out of the whole system. When companies fail to pay fair wages to entry-level workers they may save money in the short term, but it eats away at the fabric of society. And it undercuts the ability to create long term business success.

This is personal for me. I'm one of the lucky few of my generation to see the American dream work for me and my family. My grandparents emigrated to the United States from Ireland in the early decades of the last century. My grandfather started as a janitor and carpenter and my grandmother as a nanny. They firmly believed that if they worked hard and played by the rules their children and grandchildren would have the chance for a much better life.

That dream worked out for the Driscolls and many others because the United States worked differently then than it does today. There used to be an implicit social contract in the United States that if you worked hard and played by the rules, you could get ahead. That contract, like all social contracts, was imperfect and unfinished—marginalized groups never completely shared in the same way from the benefits of their labor. Nonetheless, for many workers and countless immigrants, that contract paid off in better jobs and higher pay. That social contract started to shred when full-time workers fell further and further behind as real wages declined in value. Millions are working harder and paid less, running up a down escalator that speeds up every year.

Executives who treat their low-wage workers as disposable cogs in their business machine are grinding their businesses down from the inside. The "Amazon model" of extracting as much efficiency out of an individual as possible, while paying as little as possible, undermines the future of democratic capitalism. We need to move beyond the idea that problems facing workers are just "worker problems," and start understanding that those workers are the backbone of our companies and our economy. Exploiting them might be a quick recipe for higher quarterly profits, but it undercuts the long-term potential of both our businesses and our country when you look out over a few dozen quarters.

CareCentrix isn't alone in its success. The companies that fight the trend of exploitation wages and prioritize the well-being of their employees see clear benefits. And if we start to do this on a much larger scale, so will our economy.

A Livable Wage Is Good for Business

As of the writing of this book, the United States has gone a full fifteen years with a minimum wage of $7.25. The last time the minimum wage was raised, in 2009, President Obama had just been sworn into office, Miley Cyrus had just released "Party in the U.S.A.," and the first seasons of *Modern Family* and *Jersey Shore* aired. It was a long time ago.

Fifteen years of paralysis on the minimum-wage issue is shameful, and it's also far outside of the historical norm. We have never gone this long without an increase to the federal minimum wage since it was first introduced in 1938. The previous record was ten years, from 1997 to 2007, the last time Congress voted to increase the minimum wage.[1] That means that Congress has voted to raise the federal minimum wage just once, one single time, since 1996.

The Federal Minimum Wage
Since its Inception

Oct. 1938	Oct. 1939	Oct. 1945	Jan. 1950	Mar. 1956	Sep. 1961	Sep. 1963	Feb. 1967	Feb. 1968	May. 1974	Jan. 1975	Jan. 1976	Jan. 1978	Jan. 1979	Jan. 1980	Jan. 1981	Apr. 1990	Apr. 1991	Oct. 1996	Sep. 1997	Jul. 2007	Jul. 2008	Jul. 2009

SOURCE: U.S. Department of Labor

The minimum wage has rarely been an adequate wage, but it's now reached a point where it's failing to even come close to its intended goal of ending labor conditions "detrimental to the maintenance of the minimum standard of living necessary for health, efficiency and general well-being of workers," as laid out in the Fair Labor Standards Act.[2] Congress's passivity has left the federal wage floor to gradually weaken, as inflation erodes its purchasing power with each passing year. As the cost of living rises and wages stay the same, each hour of a minimum-wage worker's time is worth less and less. While $7.25 per hour was already inadequate in 2009, in 2024—after years of rampant inflation—it's downright disgraceful.

Over the last fifteen years, the federal minimum wage has lost about 30 percent of its purchasing power. Someone earning $7.25 per hour in 2023 earned the equivalent of just $5.12 in 2009.[3] Flipped the other way, a worker earning $7.25

per hour in July of 2009, when the minimum wage was last raised, would have to earn $10.27 per hour in June 2023 just to have the same purchasing power. This is why Republican "compromise" bills (like the one they proposed in 2021) calling for a minimum-wage increase to $10 per hour is laughably inadequate. A $10-per-hour minimum wage, when adjusted for inflation, is *lower* than the last minimum wage set by Congress in 2009. Raising the wage to $10 and calling it a day isn't a solution, it's an insult.

The Labor Department calculates what it calls the "productivity of labor." It takes the total income of our nation—also called the gross domestic product, or GDP—and divides that by the total number of hours worked in the year. This calculation produces the average income, per hour, of everyone in the country, including people working in restaurants for the minimum wage, investors who make billions of dollars in profits from their companies, and the millions of Americans in between.

Over time, productivity of labor has been going up—and going up consistently, except during the depths of the COVID-19 pandemic shutdown. That means Americans, in aggregate, are delivering more economic value per hour. Additionally, while some may call a $15 minimum wage too drastic of a change, it's much closer to historical precedent than today's wage. The current federal minimum wage, when adjusted for inflation, is more than 40 percent lower than when it was at its peak purchasing power in 1968.[4] The $1.60 that a minimum-wage worker earned in 1968 would be the equivalent of $14.03 in 2023.

Real and Nominal Value of the Minimum Wage Over Time in 2023 Dollars

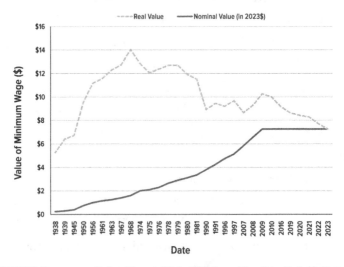

SOURCES: Department of Labor, History of Federal Minimum Wage Rates Under the Fair Labor Standards Act, 1938–2009 https://www.dol.gove/agencies/whd/minimum-wage /history/chart Bureau of Labor Statistics, CPI Inflation Calculator https://www.bls.gov/data /inflation_calculator.htm

When you consider how much worker productivity has increased over time, the stagnation of the federal minimum wage becomes even more appalling. If the minimum wage had kept pace with both inflation and productivity gains since 1968, it would be nearly $26 an hour.

Consumer Demand

Some businesspeople truly don't understand the economy. They focus on their income statements and what costs them money: labor expenses, corporate taxes, regulations, and so on. They're sitting at the top thinking about how to make that

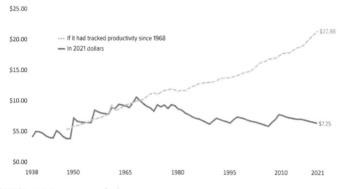

The Minimum Wage if it had kept up with Productivity, in 2021 Dollars

SOURCE: U.S. Department of Labor

mountain taller. In fact, decades of growing inequality have demonstrated without a doubt that making the top richer does not increase economic growth or help outcomes for anyone but the very rich.

We've used this failed playbook before: trickle-down economics leaves too many Americans down and out.

Our economy is not animated from the top down—it all grows from the middle and the bottom up. Seventy percent of the American economy is based on consumer demand,[5] meaning the vast majority of our country's economic activity comes from people buying things: food, clothing, electronics, cars, and Big Macs.[6] To thrive, our economy doesn't need a few more absurdly rich executives; it needs millions more customers with money in their pockets that they can freely spend.

Living on $7.25 per hour, or about $15,000 per year for a full-time worker, leaves a person with virtually no capacity

Personal Consumption Expenditures as a Percentage of Global Domestic Product

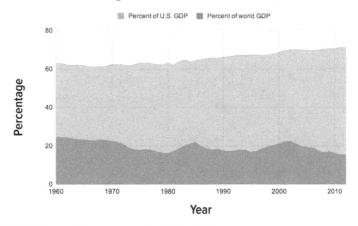

SOURCE: Bureau of Economic Analysis and World Bank

to purchase anything but the most basic necessities (and even those are often out of reach). Someone making $15,000 per year isn't eating out, or checking out new models at their local car dealership, or buying a new iPhone from Apple or new shoes from Nike. As far as those businesses are concerned, that person doesn't exist. They are essentially not much of a consumer, and at that income bracket, they will never be. People working minimum-wage jobs, or close to minimum wage, simply do not have the means to engage with most of the American economy. For people who run businesses that rely on ordinary people buying their products, this is a huge challenge.

Businesses, just like our economy, don't grow from the top down. There is no path to success with even the best executive team if your business model relies on a consumer base that cannot consume. If people can't afford to buy your product, your business will fail.

The Minimum Wage Works for All

There's a disconnect in the American business mindset that imagines the minimum-wage issue as something that only matters to minimum-wage workers. The truth is that many of the workers that pride themselves on earning more than minimum wage would see a raise from a minimum-wage increase. Yes, the few people still earning $7.25 per hour would see the most material gains from raising the minimum wage to $15 per hour—but so would people earning $10 per hour. As would the people earning $12 per hour. And there are a lot of those people.

Low-wage workers saw significant gains in the years after the pandemic. The number of people making less than $15 per hour dropped by nearly 20 million from 2019 to 2023.[7] But amid record wage gains, low-wage workers were also faced with record inflation. The number of people making less than $15 per hour might have been reduced, but $15 per hour at the end of 2019 was the equivalent of only $17.50 per hour just a few years later. The rising cost of living wiped out virtually all the gains made by workers and left those at the bottom to fall even further behind. The average low-wage worker is still a bit ahead of where they were in 2019, but barely.

As of July 2023, 19 million workers, or 14 percent of the American workforce, made less than $15 per hour. Thirty-four million, or 24 percent of the workforce, made less than $17 per hour. Fifty million, a full 35 percent of the workforce, made less than $20 per hour. There are still more than 3 million working adults who make less than $10 per hour. For context, there is no place in the entire United States where even a single adult without children can afford their basic needs on $15 per hour.[8]

Ripple Effects

There is clear evidence that raising the minimum wage also benefits workers who *already* earn more than the new wage floor. If you make $21 per hour and the minimum wage is increased to $20 per hour, the odds are pretty solid that you're going to get some kind of raise as well.

Workers in the twenty states that use the federal minimum wage, just $7.25 per hour, are almost 50 percent more likely to earn less than $15 than workers in the thirty states with a higher minimum wage.[9] There are only seven states (plus Washington, DC) whose minimum wage is $15 per hour or more.[10] But by lifting up the floor for all workers, even a $9, $10, or $12 minimum wage makes it significantly more likely that a worker will earn more than $15 per hour. A rising tide lifts all boats—and may even help power CEO superyachts.

We see the same pattern at the federal level. When the federal government raised the minimum wage from $4.25 to $5.15 per hour in 1996 and 1997, a group of academics looked at how a large retail company (given anonymity by the researchers) responded. They found that even though the share of company employees receiving legally required wage raises was less than 10 percent, virtually the entire hourly workforce saw their wages increase by 30 to 40 percent.[11]

This isn't surprising if you think about it from a company's perspective. If you're a CEO and you have a mixed workforce of employees with some earning the minimum wage, some earning slightly more than the minimum wage, and some making a moderate amount more than that, you have to keep each of those groups of workers happy. Workers earning more than the minimum wage, with skills that are more in demand than their lower-wage counterparts, are going to expect to continue earning more than their lower-paid peers no matter what happens to the minimum wage. As an employer, you need to keep these workers satisfied with their compensation, particularly since they are likely to be harder to replace than minimum-wage workers. If you're paying a store manager $15 per hour and suddenly all the people she manages start getting paid $15 per hour, you're going to have to raise the wage for that manager as well. And if you're raising pay for store managers, you're going to have to raise it for district managers.

The closer a worker is to the minimum-wage line, the more impactful the effect, but it extends surprisingly far. One analysis found that raising the federal minimum wage to $15 per hour would indirectly raise wages for 11.6 million workers who already earn more than $15.[12] Another found that people earning up to $2.50 more than the new minimum wage would see spillover wage increases.[13] Increasing the minimum wage to $17 per hour would mean an extra 14 million workers see raises.[14]

The macroeconomic effects of raising the minimum wage, combined with increased consumer demand as people have more money to spend, extend far beyond what most people imagine. Our economy is more interconnected than ever, and the plight of the poor links inextricably to the prosperity of everyone else. We're all standing on the same floor. Some of us might have found stools to stand a bit higher than others, or ladders to climb even higher, but each of those implements is still resting on the same foundation. By lifting that floor, we're not just lifting up all the people standing on solid ground—we're raising the baseline for everyone, allowing all of us to reach just a bit higher.

Higher Minimum Wages Help Companies

Of course, paying workers more means employers will be spending more money. But paying millions of workers more to buy more products and services also translates into more total profits for the economy. It's simple math. The correct thing to do as a business is not to exclusively look at payroll and see only expenses, but to consider fair pay as an investment. In most cases, companies end up better off with a higher minimum wage. The cost of paying workers more is far outweighed by the benefits of having a larger and more affluent consumer base. If this still seems too incredible to believe, let's consider an example.

Imagine you own a bar in a small town in New Hampshire. (Fun fact: New Hampshire is the state with the highest alcohol consumption per capita in the United States, so you're starting off on a strong foot already.)[15] You have one bartender, and

Workers have
more money
to spend

Pay
Workers
More

Workers spend
more money at
your business

Profit

your bar can fit about seventy-five people on a very busy night.
As a business owner, do you think you're better off keeping the
minimum wage in your town low just so you can avoid paying
your one bartender an extra $5 per hour? Or do you think that
you're better off with a higher minimum wage that both makes
it more likely people have enough money to come to your bar in

the first place, and gives the people in your bar more disposable income to spend on drinks? If that minimum-wage increase means that you sell a bit more alcohol—even just two or three more drinks per hour—you're coming out ahead.

Most small business owners agree. Despite the widespread notion that the business community is united against minimum-wage increases, 67 percent of small business owners support raising the minimum wage and indexing it to automatically increase every year.[16] As small business owners, they have a much more intimate understanding than corporate CEOs of the kinds of people who buy from their stores or eat at their restaurants. Smaller business owners see the business benefits of higher pay and more disposable income every day.

Even the largest businesses stand to gain from higher minimum wages. They might have more workers to pay, but they have even more to gain from both their workers and other low-wage workers having more money in their pockets to spend. It's easy to look at Apple, or Nike, or any other successful company and say that they seem to be doing just fine. Survivorship bias, where we only see the success stories on the Fortune 500 list, blinds us to the fact that our economy is running a race with a broken foot.

By paying over a third of American workers barely enough to survive or to engage in the economy as consumers, we shortchange businesses that rely on workers' spending. There are countless businesses, both big and small, that suffer because there are not enough consumers who can afford their products.

Consider what happened to consumer spending and businesses during the Great Recession from 2007 to 2009. Those two years were disasters for the economy. Disposable income dropped by 6 percent.[17] Consumer spending dropped 4 percent. Those are small numbers, but in the business world, they were earth-shattering.

If a drop in consumer spending of just 4 percent was enough to push our economy to the edge, imagine how damaging it is to have more than 30 percent of Americans unable to spend almost anything in the broader economy. Because we're unwilling to pay our workforce fairly, we are effectively suppressing consumer demand. It's an undeniable fact that our economy is running on partial power. That's why raising the minimum wage is an opportunity for workers and business owners alike: it would be a clear economic stimulus, giving tens of millions of consumers more money to spend in their local communities.

None of this is necessarily a new idea. It's a direct callback to the most successful economic agenda in American history: the New Deal. Coming out of the depths of the Great Depression, FDR and his advisers knew that some sort of fundamental change to the economy was needed. They bet that by lifting up the poorest workers, rather than funneling more wealth to the top, they would create a stable floor that would lead to broadly shared prosperity for all. As FDR said in a speech in 1933, "Throughout industry, the change from starvation wages and starvation employment to living wages and sustained employment can, in large part, be made by an industrial covenant to which all employers shall subscribe. It is greatly to their interest to do this because decent living, widely spread among our 125,000,000 people, eventually means the opening up to industry of the richest market which the world has known." [18]

It was a risk. But they were right. Their investments led to economic stability for millions, a growing middle class full of consumers with money to spend, and, eventually, the economic boom of the 1940s, '50s, and '60s, widely considered the golden age for the American economy. As time passed, and the New Deal was undermined by trickle-down economics and a broken Congress, inequality grew and the economy destabilized again.

We Know This Works

As you're going to see in the coming pages, nothing about the argument in favor of a higher minimum wage is based on speculation. Right-wing politicians claim that raising the minimum wage will lead to business failure, jobs lost, and the economy tanking, but we don't just think that they're wrong— we *know* that they're wrong. We don't have to guess what will happen when we raise the minimum wage, and we don't have to rely on unprovable economic models or theoretical calculations. We have dozens of pieces of evidence from across the country, countless case studies of cities and states raising their minimum wages independently of the federal floor, and they all show that raising the minimum wage ends up being overwhelmingly positive for nearly everyone.

As of March 2024, thirty-one states had minimum wages above the federal line of $7.25 an hour. [19] Thirty of those (including Washington, DC) had minimum wages above $10 an hour. Seventeen had minimum wages of at least $13 per hour, and

The Minimum Wage as of January 2024

										ME $14.15
								VT $13.67	NH $7.25	
WA $15.28	ID $7.25	MT $10.30	ND $7.25	MN $10.85	IL $14.00	WI $7.25	MI $10.33	NY $15.00	RI $14.00	MA $15.00
OR $14.20	NV $11.25	WY* $5.15	SD $11.20	IA $7.25	IN $7.25	OH $10.45	PA $7.25	NJ $15.13	CT $15.69	
CA $16.00	UT $7.25	CO $14.42	NE $12.00	MO $12.30	KY $7.25	WV $8.75	VA $12.00	MD $15.00	DE $13.25	
	AZ $14.35	NM $12.00	KS $7.25	AR $11.00	TN* $0.00	NC $7.25	SC* $0.00	DC $17.00		
			OK $7.25	LA* $0.00	MS* $0.00	AL* $0.00	GA $5.15			
AK $11.73	HI $14.00		TX $7.25					FL $12.00		

*States without a minimum wage or a minimum wage lower than $7.25 adhere to the federal minimum wage ($7.25).

SOURCE: U.S. Department of Labor, State Minimum Wage Laws https://www.dol.gov/agencies/whd/minimum-wage/state

nine had a minimum wage of at least $15 per hour in some portion or all of the state (New York and Oregon have lower minimums for rural counties). If the claims of the minimum-wage opponents are right, those states would be lagging far behind their counterparts that allow businesses to only pay $7.25. But they're not. States like Connecticut, New York, California, and Massachusetts, each with a minimum wage of at least $15 per hour, are some of the most economically vibrant states in the nation, something that comes in large part from, not in spite of, their commitment to paying workers fairly.

Don't just take it from us—take it directly from the heads of the corporate restaurant chains that have long been fighting against raising wages. On earnings call after earnings call, these CEOs have admitted to investors that a higher minimum wage is *better* for business. In fact, in 2021, the chief financial officer of Denny's was caught on a call telling investors that California's minimum-wage increase *helped* the chain's restaurants in that state outperform the rest of the country. He noted that as the minimum wage gradually increased in California, Denny's restaurants in the state saw higher sales growth and higher customer growth than in other states. As workers across California earned more, they could spend more in restaurants, including Denny's!

Despite their own positive experience with a higher minimum wage, Denny's executives are still fighting to prevent wage increases. The company continues to lobby against a $15 federal minimum wage in a move that many, including a number of shareholders, claim is a clear violation of their fiduciary duty to prioritize the company's financial well-being.[20]

Thankfully, some large companies are thinking more strategically. In 2019, McDonald's announced that it would no longer lobby against increasing the minimum wage at the local, state, or federal level.[21] McDonald's CEO Chris Kempczinski told investors that the company had gone through enough minimum-wage hikes at the state level to see that they weren't really a problem for business, and that if the federal minimum wage were raised, "McDonald's will do just fine." The chief financial officer of Six Flags, Sandeep Reddy, made similar comments during an earnings call in 2021. "To the extent that there are minimum wage increases in certain of our demographics where we operate, that has got a halo effect on the revenue side," said Reddy. The company's CEO, Michael Spanos, quickly added, "We think it absolutely helps in that regard [to] put more money in their pockets." Halo effect. How's that for a ringing endorsement for higher wages?

Business leaders who oppose raising the minimum wage might be loud and powerful, but they are increasingly in the minority. The U.S. Chamber of Commerce, the self-proclaimed voice of business in America, actively and aggressively lobbies against raising the minimum wage. You might think that means the members of the Chamber of Commerce, and the business community as a whole, oppose minimum-wage increases, but you'd be wrong.

In 2016, the Chamber conducted an internal poll of a thousand executives of its member organizations, asking them whether they thought raising the minimum wage would be a good idea. Chamber leadership was obviously hoping for a big, scary number they could shop around to reporters showing that the business community thought raising wages was a terrible idea. Instead, they got the opposite. A full *80 percent* of executives said they supported raising their state's minimum wage.[22]

What did the Chamber's leadership do with this information? Instead of taking a moment to assess why they're spending millions lobbying against something that 80 percent of their members support, they decided to pretend like it never happened. They hid the poll and, to this day, continue to fight against minimum-wage increases. The only reason the American public knows the truth is because someone inside the organization leaked it.

It seems like malpractice for the voice of the American business community to fight so hard against something that most of its members support, but the truth is, the Chamber of Commerce doesn't care what most of its 3 million members think. It exists primarily as a lobbying arm for a small number of multinational corporations (which disproportionately employ low-wage workers), and anything that conflicts with what those companies want is swept under the rug. It's convenient to be able to point to a wide breadth of businesses to improve the group's credibility, but they have little influence over what the Chamber says or does.

The majority of the Chamber's funding comes from a small group of corporations and donors who call the shots. In 2021, almost half the organization's funding came from companies giving $1 million or more annually to the Chamber, and just eighteen donors combined to account for more than a quarter of the Chamber's revenue.[23] The Chamber does not disclose its donors, but it's not hard to guess who's giving the most—the people and corporations who stand to benefit from misleading the public on the supposed unpopularity of a minimum-wage increase.

Stephen Prince's Story

Stephen Prince is the founder and owner of Card Market Services.

My wife and I started our printing company on September 12, 1993, with only two goals. The first was standard for most entrepreneurs, and an absolute nonnegotiable: be profitable. I'm a proud capitalist, and I like making money. I firmly believe that without a profit and success motive, there would be no United States of America. The ability to achieve financial success and all the accoutrements that go with it is a driving force in our capitalistic nation.

The second goal is where I depart, unfortunately, from most of my fellow capitalists: to do good with my money—for my employees, most of all, and for *humankind in general*. I don't think that making a lot of money is incompatible with having concern for others. I don't need to live in a tent to prove that I care about the less fortunate. I can do good and live comfortably at the same time.

For business owners and executives, doing good has to start with the employees who make your own success possible. As much as some self-proclaimed business "geniuses" might hate to admit it, no one can reach any real level of success on their own. I certainly didn't. It didn't take long for Carol, my wife and partner, and I to realize that our growing printing business needed help soon after we started. I was making sales calls all over the country, and she alone couldn't do all the support work that needed to be done, such as sourcing, quoting, and art development. We hired an accounting person to help with billing and financials. Before long, we hired another salesperson, which resulted in the need for more support staff. Before you knew it, we outgrew our living room and had to move into real offices. Then the back-office work really began—taking care of our employees.

Being an employer is a big responsibility, and one Carol and I took seriously. We went to great lengths to make sure that our employees were paid well and that they were offered excellent benefits, especially health care. Too many business owners look at health care and other benefits as unnecessary expenses, but I think if you want to be successful, you must take care of your employees. Personally, I think it's absurd that businesses are on the hook for providing medical care for their employees—that should be the government's job—but until we restructure our health care system, it's up to employers to provide solid health care to their workers.

If we, as business owners and operators, provide our employees with the comfort of knowing that they'll be taken care of if they or anyone in their family falls ill, they'll be happier, healthier people and better employees because of it. The same goes for pay—if we pay workers enough to feel secure, they're going to be happier, less distracted by the problems that accompany poverty, and more focused on their work. People who have never had to worry about paying for health care or being late on their rent have no appreciation of how that becomes an eternally and ever-present dark cloud over one's head. It's easy for an employer to be so focused on the money in their own pocket, or in their shareholders' brokerage accounts, that they lose sight of the ground-level things that make success possible.

Well-paid, appreciated employees are by far the better foundation to build a company on than frightened, downtrodden employees. I've seen this in both my business and in others we've worked with, like Costco. One of the founders of Costco, Jim Sinegal, was often recognized as a benevolent, employee-centric leader. He was never paid the millions of dollars in annual salaries and bonuses that most large corporations pay their executives, but he retired as a billionaire in 2012 as the value of Costco's stock was beginning to grow. Most other CEOs of publicly traded companies want both: huge salaries and benefits, as well as the stock options. That way, if they do a bad job of running the company and the stock doesn't perform well, then they still get their wealth in the form of exorbitant salaries and bonuses. Not at Costco. Jim's theory was that "we're all in this together."

About fifteen years ago, Carol and I flew to the West Coast and met with the Costco team. We were able to set up a relationship that exists to this day, partly because of what we found there: employees that were happy and satisfied with their jobs. After all, salaries and benefits at Costco are excellent, and the employee turnover there is so low it's virtually nonexistent. Costco became a global juggernaut, and Jim Sinegal became a billionaire—not in spite of the company's employees, but because of them. Treating your workers well is the best long-term way to do capitalism right.

The bottom line from my perspective is simple: a business built and operated around a principle of sharing and concern for your employees, your customers, your country, and your community will always accrue value to you, the owner-operator. Paying a living wage, paying taxes (the fuel of a nation's engine) and operating your enterprise with the long view, beyond your own life and needs, is a winning formula for success and happiness.

The State of the Minimum Wage

Realistically, we're still a long way from a minimum wage that meets even the bare minimum for what workers need to survive. Even if a minimum-wage bill were passed immediately, it would be years before it was fully phased in. What should businesses do in the meantime, while they're still only legally required to pay $7.25 an hour? Simple: they should pay their workers more because it's better for their business.

When an employee makes so little that she can't afford her rent and is sleeping in her car, of course it will have an impact on her work. When employees are chronically stressed about paying their bills, they are distracted on the job and their work suffers. If an employee is unable to afford to treat a health condition, they are going to be both mentally distracted and physically compromised on the job, and their work will be negatively affected.

This isn't hypothetical. Across the economy, surveys show that more than half of workers spend three or more working hours per week dealing with or thinking about issues related to their personal finances.[1] Those are hours they're not performing at their best, and removing that stressor means more than just happier employees—it means more productivity, and more profits.

Researchers consistently see a connection between happy employees and successful businesses. A 2019 study by the London School of Economics found that employee satisfaction, measured by survey questions like, "How satisfied are you with your organization as a place to work?," was directly correlated with not just employee productivity but business profitability.[2] The benefits didn't stop there. Higher employee satisfaction was also found to be associated with higher customer loyalty. This makes logical sense—customers who regularly encounter motivated and happy employees are more likely to be happy with their experience than ones who are forced to deal with stressed and burnt-out employees.

The connection even extends to the one area that most corporate executives obsess about—stock prices. The companies that were listed in the "100 Best Companies to Work for in America" from 1984 to 2011 had reliably better returns on the stock market than their competitors. Their stock prices experienced an average annual growth 2.3–3.8 percent higher than their peers who weren't on the list.[3]

None of this should come as a surprise, but too many executives look at their low-wage workers as numbers on a spreadsheet, not as individuals with interior lives just as meaningful as their own. Coming to grips with the humanity of the workforce might not be something that's often taught in business school, but ensuring that employees are able to provide for themselves and their families is one of the most important changes a company can make if it really wants to maximize productivity.

Turning Over a New Leaf

One challenge facing every executive is employee turnover. Replacing a current employee with a new one is a frustrating and expensive part of doing business. One of the key indicators of a healthy, well-run company is low turnover numbers—the fewer people that leave, the better a company tends to do. On the flip side, the more employees that leave, the less productive your company tends to be.

Paying your workers fairly and treating them well leads, unsurprisingly, to increased employee retention. The happier and better paid your workers are, the less likely they are to leave for another job with a better work environment or pay. This is one of the biggest benefits of paying employees better.

We can see firsthand the effect that the minimum wage has on employee retention by looking at state-by-state data. The hiring rates of red states, according to research by the *Washington Post*, were considerably higher than those of blue states for at least a ten-year span.[4] This might sound like a good

Hiring, Quitting, and Firing by State

State	Hire Rate	Layoff/Fire Rate	Quit Rate	2020 Election
Alaska	5.8%	1.8%	3.0%	Trump
Montana	5.3%	1.7%	3.1%	Trump
Wyoming	4.7%	1.3%	2.7%	Trump
Idaho	4.5%	1.5%	2.4%	Trump
Louisiana	4.5%	1.4%	2.7%	Trump
Arkansas	4.4%	1.1%	2.6%	Trump
South Carolina	4.4%	1.2%	2.8%	Trump
Oklahoma	4.3%	1.2%	2.4%	Trump
West Virginia	4.3%	1.1%	3.1%	Trump
Florida	4.2%	0.9%	2.6%	Trump
Illinois	3.4%	0.9%	2.0%	Biden
Maryland	3.4%	1.6%	2.2%	Biden
Hawaii	3.2%	1.3%	1.7%	Biden
Michigan	3.1%	0.8%	1.5%	Biden
Washington	3.1%	0.9%	1.7%	Biden
Wisconsin	3.1%	1.0%	2.2%	Biden
California	3.0%	0.9%	1.7%	Biden
New York	3.0%	0.9%	1.8%	Biden
Massachusetts	2.9%	0.8%	1.6%	Biden
Pennsylvania	2.9%	0.7%	1.8%	Biden

SOURCE: Bureau of Labor Statistics

thing, but it came with no significant difference in job growth or economic development, measured by indicators like new start-ups and new housing permits.

Instead, the difference in hiring rates can be attributed to one factor: quitting. The difference in hiring numbers between red and blue states almost perfectly matches the difference in how many workers quit their jobs each year. Red states, with lower minimum wages and fewer worker protections, see significantly higher turnover and considerably lower employee retention. In every single one of the last twenty-five years, workers in states won by Trump in 2020 spent anywhere from 0.2 to 0.5 fewer years in their jobs than workers in states won by Biden.[5]

Biden States Average Growth
vs. Trump State Average Growth

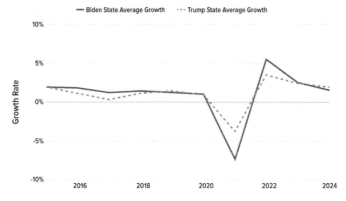

SOURCE: Bureau of Labor Statistics

This trend tracks across every industry, from the most transient, like retail, to the most stable, like education or government work. However, it doesn't track across income groups, as higher earners tend to spend more time in their jobs in red states. The difference is largely concentrated among the lowest-income, least-educated workers—exactly the type of workers whom the higher minimum wages and worker protections in blue states are meant to help.

Wages for the lowest-paid workers have remained so abysmal that employers in industries with a high number of low-wage workers have been conditioned to take high turnover for granted. Half of employers in a *Harvard Business Review* survey estimated that turnover for their low-wage workforce was over 24 percent each year, and nearly a quarter thought it was higher than 50 percent.[6] But here's the thing: for the most part, low-wage workers do not choose jobs they want to quit; they actively *want* to stay in their current jobs. They look for better prospects elsewhere when they figure out that their employers don't value them or pay them as much as they deserve.

Just like businesses, workers value familiarity and stability. Changing jobs is stressful and full of uncertainty for everyone, but especially low-wage workers. What if their new boss is a jerk? What if the working conditions are worse than they seem from the outside? There are lots of unknowns that most people would avoid, if given the chance. But when faced with the certainty of working in an underpaid, under-respected role, the unknown often seems like the better option. If given the opportunity to grow in their current positions, however, most workers would choose to stay.

In that same *Harvard Business Review* survey, 62 percent of low-wage workers said that getting a raise or a promotion would make them more likely to stay with their current employer. Nine percent said they'd be more likely to stay even with the same pay if their employer gave them more skills training, and 6 percent said they'd stay if given more responsibility. Twenty-two percent said that they would prefer to stay in their current jobs even without any changes to their pay, training, or responsibilities.

Yet while some workers want more responsibility or are content to stay in their current jobs, the most significant impact on employee retention is pay. Compensation is the number one reason why employees leave a job, with 55 percent of resignations being driven by pay increases.[7] This is true across job categories, but is particularly prevalent for lower-paid workers. $25 per hour seems to be the point at which compensation becomes not quite as important, but below that, every dollar makes a real difference in a business's ability to retain its workers.[8]

The workers paid the absolute lowest wage are also the ones most likely to quit at any given time, making any business model that relies on minimum-wage work inherently unstable. In 2019, data from employers showed that workers earning the federal minimum wage were more than twice as likely to quit their jobs as workers making the national average.[9] Workers earning $7.25 an hour had a greater than 70 percent chance of leaving their job within a year. Raise that number to $15, however, and their turnover rate drops down to only 42 percent. At $20 an hour, that number dropped even further to 35 percent.

How Hourly Wage Impacts Turnover

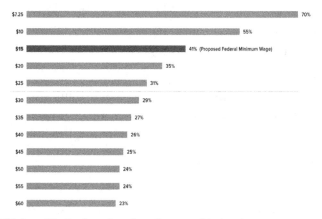

SOURCE: Gusto, Why Employees Leave https://gusto.com/blog/people-management/why-employees-leave

Costs of Employee Turnover

Replacing an employee, even a low-level one, is expensive. There are direct expenses related to turnover, like hiring recruiters and training, that are easily trackable on balance sheets, and there are more indirect costs, like loss of productivity for staff who need to cover for an absence. All these costs can add up to thousands of dollars per employee, if not more.

The absolute lowest estimate of the cost to replace a single employee that can be found in any business study is somewhere around 33 percent of an employee's annual salary.[10] Someone making $21,000 per year costs $7,000 to replace. Someone making $45,000 per year costs $15,000. Even replacing someone making barely more than the minimum wage, just $8 per hour, ends up costing companies an average of $3,500.[11] That's the equivalent of 437 hours of lost work at that wage, or almost 55 days of full-time work. If a company were to instead give that worker a $2-per-hour raise to keep them on board, it would take 218 days of full-time work, almost an entire year, just to spend that $3,500.

Thirty-three percent of an employee's annual pay is significant, but by most experts' opinions, the real number is much higher. Some put the real cost at somewhere between 50 percent and 200 percent of an employee's annual compensation, and predict that for the average company with a hundred employees, turnover costs can reach up to $2.6 million per year.[12] One even higher estimate in the *Harvard Business Review* puts the cost of replacing an employee at between 100 percent and 300 percent of that employee's entire annual salary.[13] That's right—sometimes it's theoretically more profitable for a company to double an employee's salary than to replace them every year.

Even in industries with comparatively low replacement costs, employee turnover is a serious expense. The Center for Hospitality Research at Cornell University studied employee turnover in the restaurant industry and found that replacing a single employee costs an average of $5,864.[14] Given turnover rates, that means the average restaurant will spend something in the realm of $150,000 each year because of employee turnover.

The average cost breakdown looks like this:

```
****************************
      Employee Turnover
****************************
Average              Cost Breakdown
-------------------------------------

Pre-departure
loss of productivity         $176

Recruitment                $1,173

New hire selection           $645

Orientation & training       $821

Productivity loss          $3,049
-------------------------------------


TOTAL AMOUNT       $5,864.00



-------------------------------------

******** THANK YOU! ********
```

SOURCE: Center for Hospitality Research, Cornell University, http://scholarship.sha.cornell.edu/cgi/viewcontent.cgi?article=1148&context=chrpubs

As these numbers make clear, productivity loss is the most significant expense associated with employee turnover. Unfortunately, it's also one of the trickiest for individual companies to measure. A job doesn't just disappear in the time between when a person quits and their replacement is hired. You can't look at how much work that one person did every day and write it off as lost productivity during the gap. Instead, that job's responsibilities are more likely spread across other employees, who will likely do a worse job without as much specific expertise, while also having less time and energy to do their own jobs. Managers, too, will have to devote a significant amount of their time to hiring a replacement, taking away from the bandwidth they have available to help their existing team run smoothly and efficiently.

Additionally, there is some level of institutional knowledge lost when an employee leaves a company. Executives tend to only consider this a real problem at the top level of business, where losing other executives or professional staff leads to obvious gaps in knowledge, but it can be equally impactful with low-wage workers. Losing the employee who knows where everything in the storage closet is located, or the cook who is the only one who can get the wonky burner to turn on, or the one who used to teach all the new hires the most efficient path to stock shelves might seem minor at first, but it's the small efficiencies that make workplaces run smoothly. When you take out the people who are the grease on the wheels of your business, you're going to get jammed gears.

Regardless of how much the rest of the business relies on them, losing an employee who knows how the place works and replacing that person with someone who doesn't is inevitably going to result in some lost productivity. A new hire is simply not going to be as productive right away as the person they're replacing. It takes time to get fully trained, and even after official training is over, it takes even longer to get the hang of a job well enough to do it efficiently. No matter how simple a job is, no one is as productive on their fifth day as they are on their five hundredth day.

The exact amount of time varies by industry and position, but in general, it takes workers much more time to reach peak productivity than you might think. Some estimates put the average "time to productivity"—or TTP, as it's known in the business world—at anywhere from eight months, to ten months, to one year, to a full two years![15] Not everyone is going to take two years to get fully up to speed, but even when considering the most conservative estimates, that's a significant stretch of time for a position not be as productive as possible. If, based on expert estimates, the average worker spends just four years at one job, you're looking at subpar productivity nearly 25 percent of the time.[16]

Companies and industries with high turnover rates have it even worse. At fast-food restaurants, for instance, it takes about four months for an employee to reach an expected level of productivity.[17] That's significantly below the average for most other jobs, so you'd think it'd be easier for fast-food companies to run at full productivity. But more than 50 percent of fast-food employees quit before they reach even three months on the job.[18] At any given time, a fast-food restaurant likely has more than half its staff working below peak productivity.

It's easy to underestimate the importance of experience when it comes to jobs that people think of as "low skill" positions. But even in environments where individual expertise is deliberately devalued, like factory assembly lines, high employee turnover can have serious effects on both productivity and product quality.

This is an old problem. As Henry Ford started ramping up production of his Model T cars in 1913, he faced rampant absenteeism and high employee turnover.[19] Ford's use of an assembly line, where workers performed one specialized task all day, every day, was a breakthrough when it came to efficiency, but it was also extremely boring. Not everyone wanted to work on a monotonous assembly line doing the same simple task for ten hours a day. Ford decided to tackle the problem with a simple solution that many modern businessmen could learn from: he paid his workers more. In 1914, Ford more than doubled his minimum wage, from $2.25 to $5 per day (the equivalent of a modern-day $17-per-hour wage), and saw the benefits almost immediately. Productivity soared, turnover plummeted, and Ford Motor Company doubled its profits in less than two years. (A commonly shared but technically untrue piece of this story is that Ford decided to pay his workers more to ensure they could afford the cars they were producing, thus increasing his base of consumers. That was a very happy by-product of Ford's decision to raise wages, but it wasn't the actual reason.)

Morale

It's not just short-term losses of productivity that businesses need to worry about. High turnover will have serious long-term consequences for the culture of an organization (and every good executive knows that building a strong company culture is critical to company success).

High turnover doesn't just make it difficult to build a cohesive culture; it erodes what already exists. When employees quit, they take institutional knowledge with them, and they also leave behind a more unstable workforce. High turnover can be a *symptom* of low employee morale, but it's also a major cause. When workers leave, the ones who stay behind feel worse about their jobs, both on a professional and personal level.

In most cases, it's hard to fill a job immediately. Meanwhile, the work that was done by an employee who's no longer there still exists. What happens, then, is that the employees who stick around take on extra work—usually without extra pay—which is a potent recipe for burnout. Beyond increases in workload, the loss of coworkers often has a profound effect on an employee's satisfaction with their job. The number one reason most Americans report loving their jobs, above the work itself or their work-life balance, is their coworkers.[20] That's a good thing, because most people spend eight hours a day, five days a week, with their coworkers. That's more time than many spend with their families! All those hours together help coworkers develop deep bonds. Not everyone is going to be friends, but socializing with coworkers is often one of the more pleasant parts of a person's workday.

Just as those bonds can help strengthen a company's culture and encourage workers to stay and give their best, they do the opposite when the bonds are broken. It's miserable to work in a job and have your friends regularly leave. All the inside jokes, the meals together where you light-heartedly complain about your boss, the drinks after work—they made work fun. When they disappear, each day feels a little grayer, and just a bit harder to get through. It's even more miserable when you then have to pick up more work for little extra pay, potentially for months, and then train their replacements. Even after those roles are filled, an employee in a high-turnover workplace can start to feel like a stranger among their own team as the people they got to know when they started move on. It becomes easier to start imagining yourself moving on as well.

That's another problem with employee turnover—it's contagious. The more that people quit, the more the remaining employees start to think about leaving. Increased workload and loss of coworker relationships can push people to look elsewhere, which puts more strain on the workers who remain, who then are more likely to quit themselves. It's a vicious cycle that can strip a company's workforce bare if executives aren't careful.

Scheduling

Low wages aren't the only business practice that, driven by a desire to pay workers as little as possible and keep overhead costs low, undermines a company's ability to keep their workers motivated and productive. We've also got to talk about how companies schedule their hourly workers.

To keep labor costs down, many companies hire part-time

hourly employees instead of full-time ones (because you don't have to offer as many benefits to part-time employees, and they're less able to negotiate for higher pay). While salaried employees typically have a consistent schedule, something like the classic 9 to 5, Monday through Friday timetable, hourly employees often work unpredictable hours that change week by week, including in the number of hours they are given.

Managers shuffle hours around every week to provide adequate service to their customers, and (hopefully) to keep employees as happy as possible. Contrary to all those reports about people not wanting to work anymore, polls of service workers consistently show that more than half want to work more hours.[21] Obviously, some shifts are more desirable than others, and managers often give workers different schedules each week, aiming to spread the pain around rather than make any specific workers unhappy.

"Clopenings," or working a closing shift at a store and then working the opening shift the very next day, are common, leaving workers with just a couple hours to sleep in between.[22] So are "on-call" shifts, where an employee isn't necessarily scheduled to work, but must be available to work if their supervisor decides extra hands are needed, with at best a few hours of warning before being called in.[23]

Workers often learn their schedules at the last minute. In fact, two-thirds of service workers receive their schedules less than two weeks in advance.[24] This type of scheduling creates a tremendous amount of uncertainty for hourly workers. For one, it's awfully hard to pick up hours at a second job if you don't know when you are going to be needed at your first job. Inconsistent work schedules lead to inconsistent sleep schedules and prevent people from planning for routine family obligations, like picking their child up from school at the same time every week. Even worse, an inconsistent number of hours can leave workers with wide fluctuations in their week-to-week income. According to a sample of reports from hourly workers, between the weeks with the most hours worked and those with the fewest, there is a 32 percent difference in hours worked.[25]

Trying to negotiate this imbalance would be difficult for anyone, but it's particularly challenging for parents, and a total nightmare for single parents. Today nearly 30 percent of American families are headed by a single parent.[26] That's over 10 million people raising over 18 million children.[27] How does anyone financially plan when in any given week their income could be a third lower than it was the week before? Childcare is expensive, and placing a child in a daycare often requires months-long commitments. Not being able to plan for essential tasks a few weeks out—your childcare needs, your pickup schedule, your bill payments—is a recipe for disaster.

All of this combines to make life supremely difficult for millions of hourly workers in America, although it isn't just a problem for workers. In what has become a pattern for many in the business community, the relentless pursuit of short-term profits and cost cutting ends up hurting businesses as well. If your employees are tired and stressed out about whether they can afford to live on their wages, much less pick

Low-wage workers have high rates of low-quality schedules
Percentage of U.S. food and retail workers that experience each type of scheduling problem

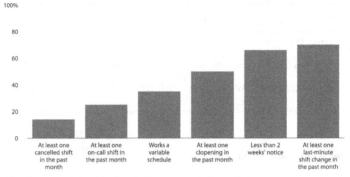

NOTE: Clopening shifts are back-to-back opening and closing shifts.
SOURCE: Author's tabulations from the Shift Project survey.

Equitable Growth

up their kid from school, they're not going to be able to do their best for the company.

When companies have experimented with more consistent scheduling, they have universally seen significant improvements in worker happiness and, most importantly for their bottom line, worker productivity. Higher scheduling stability has been shown to increase worker productivity by up to 24 percent.[28] Even in more customer service–oriented roles, where productivity is harder to measure, the benefits are clear. When a group of GAP stores started giving employees more stable schedules, sales at those stores increased by an average of 3.3 percent.[29]

Higher schedule stability can also mitigate high employee turnover. Businesses are damaging themselves by making their workers suffer through sleep problems, stress, financial instability, and family conflicts—things that are unsustainable even for the most committed employees. Workers can't maintain such a difficult lifestyle for long, which explains why inconsistent scheduling is highly correlated with increased worker turnover.[30] It's expensive and time-consuming to constantly train new employees to replace the ones that quit. It's much easier and cheaper to adjust working schedules to give your current employees more reasons to stay.

Debunking Myths

Corporate America's preternatural ability to make bad decisions is surpassed only by its talent for inventing reasons why those bad decisions are actually good. This is particularly true when it comes to executives justifying low pay for millions of people (and outsized compensation for themselves). Executives insist that there are "business" reasons for underpaying employees. While they may occasionally admit that workers are not paid enough, they will often couple that confession with dire warnings about what will happen if such circumstances change.

According to some top executives, paying employees something they might be able to live on will destroy business, the economy, and perhaps civilization, in that order. Business leaders are afforded a great deal of respect in our country, particularly by politicians and the media. It's easy to understand why, as a society, we have continued to accept the way things are—but rest assured, nothing is going to collapse if we pay people fairly for the work they do. Quite the opposite. In fact, let's go through some of corporate America's favorite justifications for low pay. (Spoiler alert: they do not stand up to scrutiny.)

Myth #1: Raising the minimum wage will force businesses, especially small businesses, to close.

Evidence overwhelmingly contradicts this assertion. Minimum-wage increases don't hurt businesses, they *help* them. Remember the Denny's executive who admitted to investors that California's minimum-wage increase helped the company's California locations become more profitable? The same is true for businesses of all sizes. Research shows that small businesses in states with higher minimum wages grow faster than their counterparts in states with minimum wages of $7.25 per hour.[1] It's easier for them to hire workers, it's easier for them to retain workers, and they have a much more robust customer base with more money to spend.

That's on the macro level, of course. On a more granular level, there are almost certainly some businesses that would suffer if the federal minimum wage increased, and the stories of those businesses closing will certainly be trotted out by the opposition. But perhaps a small number of businesses losing while a majority of workers and businesses win is not the worst thing for business or society. And don't forget that many of those businesses whose survival depends on paying the federal minimum are also depending on your federal and state taxes to subsidize their businesses via the Medicaid and SNAP assistance (Supplemental Nutrition Assistance Program, also known as food stamps) that their workers rely on.

If your business model cannot survive without government subsidies and human suffering, it's probably not a net positive for taxpayers or the communities they serve. There is real wisdom in what President Franklin Delano Roosevelt said in a speech after signing the National Industrial Recovery Act of 1933 into law: "No business which depends for existence on paying less than living wages to its workers has any right to continue in this country. By 'business' I mean the whole of commerce as well as the whole of industry; by workers I mean all workers, the white-collar class as well as the men in overalls; and by living wages I mean more than a bare subsistence level—I mean the wages of decent living."[2]

A business's right to exist isn't absolute. If you can't make it work while also paying your employees enough to live on, then you may not have a good business. You certainly don't deserve to have employees.

Myth #2: The minimum wage is only a starter wage for teenagers; it's not something people need to survive.

Many people imagine that every minimum-wage worker is a pimply-faced teenager trying to earn some spending money so that they can go to the mall with their friends on the week-end. Those people aren't just wrong, they're wrong on two accounts—teens don't go to malls anymore, and more importantly, they are not the majority demographic working minimum wage.[3] The average age for a low-wage worker is thirty-five years old; over a third are in their forties or older, and more than a quarter of this group have children to support. Only about 17 percent of minimum-wage workers are teenagers.[4] The popular belief that a low-wage job is simply a "starter" job to get someone experience before they find a "real" job is fantasy. Career mobility, particularly for workers making the least amount of money, is today less a realistic aspiration and more of a pipe dream.

Millions of Americans from all walks of life work minimum-wage jobs. As of April 2023, 19 million workers, or 14 percent of the American workforce, made less than $15 per hour; 34 million, or 24 percent of the workforce, made less than $17 per hour; and 50 million, a full 35 percent of the workforce, made less than $20 per hour. There are still more than 3 million working adults who make less than $10 per hour.[5]

These are not interns and students auditioning for a career; in fact, many Americans work low-wage jobs their entire lives. The *Harvard Business Review* found, after tracking over 181,000 people who took low-wage jobs in 2012, that more than 60 percent of them were still in low-wage jobs years later.[6] Some had given up and exited the workforce, some had found higher-paying jobs, but a majority were still working for about the same amount of money, in about the same type of role.

Who benefits from a higher minimum wage?

⊢ WHAT PEOPLE ⊣ THINK

Teenager

Works part time after school

Lives with parents

Earning extra spending money

⊢ THE REALITY ⊣

Average age:
35 years old

90% are not teens, they're 20 or older

59% are women

28% have children

54% work full time

Essential and front-line workers make up a majority of those who would benefit.

Statistics describe civilian workers, ages 16+, who would be affected by an increase in the federal minimum wage to $15.00 by 2025.

More at epi.org/raisethewage

Economic
Policy
Institute

Myth #3: Raising the minimum wage can decrease the earnings of low-wage workers, because businesses have to cut hours or eliminate jobs.

This is one of those arguments that sounds logical but isn't backed by evidence.

Businesses don't employ people whimsically. If a position isn't necessary to keep a business running and profitable, then that position will be eliminated no matter what the employee is being paid. Conversely, if a position is needed to keep a business running, it's probably going to be just as essential when the employee is being paid $30,000 a year instead of $15,000. A higher minimum wage might increase payroll costs for some businesses, but it doesn't make those jobs obsolete.

We don't have to speculate on this—there are dozens of case studies of states and cities raising wages without reducing employment. In fact, in many cases a higher minimum wage increases the number of available jobs as businesses expand to meet higher consumer demand.

While New York has one of the highest minimum wages in the nation, Pennsylvania is one of the few states on the East Coast that still has a $7.25-per-hour minimum wage. Moving from one state to the other as a minimum-wage worker means you can earn literally twice as much money per hour. On the flip side, moving a business across the border from New York to Pennsylvania means you can pay your workers half of what they would have made otherwise. And it's an easy trip—the two states share a land border just under 250 miles long. Many small towns exist right on the border, and some communities are split in half—one side in Pennsylvania, one in New York. This border makes for a perfect case study to test whether raising the minimum wage kills jobs.

In 2012, both New York and Pennsylvania had the exact same minimum wage: just $7.25 per hour. Since then, New York has raised its minimum wage, while Pennsylvania workers have been stuck at $7.25. Faced with the prospect of having to pay higher wages in 2013, employers across the state panicked, predicting doom for the state economy if businesses were to move en masse across the border to a state where it was cheaper to do business. But did that happen? The Federal Reserve Bank of New

York, hardly a progressive organization, says no. It performed an analysis in 2019 of employment and wage growth in two of the industries with the most low-wage workers—leisure and hospitality, and retail—and found that by almost every metric, New York ended up equal to or better than Pennsylvania.[7]

Wage growth in New York was, unsurprisingly, significantly higher than in Pennsylvania. In the leisure and hospitality industry, workers in Pennsylvania made an average of 15 percent more in 2019 than they did in 2013. Leisure and hospitality workers in New York, however, saw an increase more than twice that size, earning 33 percent more in 2019 than they did in 2013. We see a similar pattern in retail: Pennsylvania workers saw about a 10 percent increase in earnings by 2019, while the pay of New York workers increased by about 20 percent. In terms of employment numbers, the metric that business leaders promised would be horribly low because jobs would be lost, New York again ended up ahead. Both states saw basically equal losses of jobs in retail, and New York saw significantly more job growth in leisure and hospitality.

Here's the kicker: this wasn't based on statewide data. This data isn't skewed by an unfair comparison of New York City and Philadelphia. The New York Federal Reserve Bank only looked at the nineteen counties that were directly on the New York–Pennsylvania border—counties that are virtually identical, except for the fact that some of them are in one state, and the rest are in the other. We're talking about communities separated by at most just a few miles, and sometimes literally several feet. The only explanation for the stark contrast is their difference in wages.

Data Are Drawn from the Following Nineteen New York–Pennsylvania Border Counties

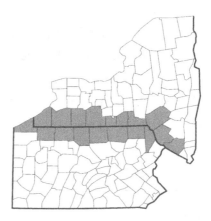

Earnings Rose More in New York than Pennsylvania Counties with No Adverse Effects on Employment

NOTES: Employment and average weekly earnings for the leisure and hospitality industry in both states are indexed to 100 in Quarter 4 2013, the quarter before New York's first minimum wage increase. The horizontal dotted line indicates the average for the nine Pennsylvania counties and the horizontal gray line indicates the average for the ten New York counties. Vertical dotted lines indicate time points in which New York's minimum wage was increased.

SOURCE: Bureau of Labor Statistics

The Federal Reserve Bank of New York published its study in 2019, when New York's rural minimum wage was just $11.80 per hour. More recent analysis of the border divide from 2022, when the state's minimum wage was $14.20 per hour, shows even more striking results.[8] New York's higher minimum wage allowed low-wage workers in the state to recover from the COVID-19 downturn more quickly, and wage gains became even more pronounced. From 2013 to 2022, earnings for leisure and hospitality workers in Pennsylvania increased by only 10 percent. In that same period, their peers in New York saw their earnings increase by almost 50 percent. New York leisure and hospitality workers on the border made on average $111 per week more than their counterparts across the border, adding up to $5,772 more over the course of a year.

Overall, it's undeniable that low-wage workers are doing better on the New York side of the border than in Pennsylvania, with basically no tradeoff when it comes to business success or employment. It's a win-win. All the fears of business collapse from New York business leaders never came to pass. The incentive for businesses to move to communities with lower wages was eliminated by the promise of higher wages in New York for employees. Businesses that moved to Pennsylvania faced a real problem: they could pay their workers less, but no one wanted to work for them for $7.25 per hour if they could make $13 per hour across the street.

The benefits of paying higher wages are so undeniable that we now see Pennsylvania business owners pressing their own legislature to raise the state's minimum wage.[9] In a 2023 interview with the *Pennsylvania Capital-Star*, John Schall, the owner of El

Jefe's Taqueria, which has locations in Pittsburgh, State College, and Bethlehem, said, "The Pennsylvania economy would be way better off if the legislation gets passed." He emphasized that higher wages across Pennsylvania would increase worker productivity by reducing turnover, saying, "In terms of just making good business sense, when people are with me for six months, a year, or a year and a half, or two years, they are way more than twice as productive than people who I just hired. Keeping staff is a really important part of my business model."

Another business owner, Amy Edelman, the proprietor of Night Kitchen Bakery in Philadelphia, made the case that higher minimum wages mean increased spending at Pennsylvania businesses. "We feel that if our employees are making a living wage and have more spending, they will spend more money in places like our bakery," Edelman said. "The American economy depends on consumer spending, that is the most important thing that keeps our economy going and healthy. If people are barely surviving, they don't have that money to keep the economy going and then the economy can collapse."

Myth #4: Raising the minimum wage will lead to increased automation, eliminating low-wage jobs entirely.

"Say goodbye to entry-level jobs and hello to permanent double-digit unemployment."

That's what Michael Saltsman, a research fellow at the Employment Policies Institute (a fake "think" tank funded by lobbyists for the restaurant and hotel industries), wrote in a

2010 op-ed criticizing Illinois lawmakers' efforts to raise the state minimum wage for fast-food workers.[10] He promised that requiring restaurants to pay their workers slightly more would result in extreme levels of automation, with "Burger-Tron 3000" replacing all the workers at McDonald's.

This claim is not only tired but untrue. Opponents make the case that raising wages will make labor so expensive that companies will be forced to automate away all the jobs that would have benefited from the raises. Workers making $7.25 per hour won't be making $15, they say—they'll be making nothing. Minimum-wage increases might seem like a good thing for low-wage workers, the argument goes, but actually it is the worst thing you could do for them.

Well, Illinois's minimum wage in 2023 was $13 an hour. In Chicago, the minimum wage for companies like McDonald's with more than twenty employees was $15.80. If Michael was right, Illinois and all the other states with high minimum wages should be experiencing permanent double-digit unemployment, right?

In 2023 Illinois's unemployment rate hovered between 4.0 and 4.5 percent.[11] Michael's doomsday prediction never came to pass.

All the evidence we have from the dozens of state and local minimum-wage increases shows that raising the minimum wage does not decrease employment in low-wage industries. Some studies do show a very small correlation between minimum-wage increases and automation. One found that for every $1 increase in the minimum wage, automatable jobs decreased by less than half of 1 percent.[12]

It is typical to expect that some jobs will become automated, but the economic stimulus derived from increased consumer demand typically creates new ones, allowing for little to no net decrease in overall jobs. One study of counties that raised their wages to $15 per hour found that those counties saw substantially higher job growth in the fast-food sector, one of the industries most susceptible to automation, than similar counties that didn't raise their minimum wage at all.[13] Other studies have found that states that already have higher minimum wages don't see lower levels of employment, and states that raise their minimum wage don't see overall decreases in employment. The macro benefits far outweigh the micro costs.

Automation Is Coming Whether We Like It or Not

"Automation" is a scary word for workers, but unfortunately, it's something we're going to have to get used to. With the development of new technologies and more advanced artificial intelligence, automation is becoming more of a reality every day, and no amount of wage stagnation will stop it. Jobs that are profitable to automate in counties and states where the minimum wage is $15 per hour today are going to be more profitable to automate at $12 per hour in a few years, and $10 per hour a few years after that. Some jobs are going to disappear forever no matter how low the minimum wage remains.

Over the last decade, many states raising their minimum wages have seen cashier positions, particularly in groceries and fast food, replaced by self-checkout machines or ordering kiosks. Watching your *job suddenly disappear is traumatic, and some workers, particularly older ones, might not fully recover from being laid off. But how much better off would they be if they spent their prior forty working years earning 30 percent more money?*

As technology makes some jobs obsolete, it also creates new ones. Carriage-makers and horse breeders were eventually replaced by automobile builders. Candlemakers were eventually replaced by lightbulb manufacturers. It's an inevitable cycle that no minimum-wage laws are going to change. But without an adequate wage floor, many of those new jobs will be just as low paying as the jobs that are eliminated. Raising the minimum wage is about more than providing fair compensation to today's workers—it's about setting a baseline for all jobs of the future and ensuring that, as our economy grows and changes, whatever jobs that do exist pay workers a fair wage.

Myth #5: This isn't an issue for the government, because the free market will naturally take care of it.

We do not have, and never had, a totally "free market." Even the biggest supporters of the free market, Wall Street bankers, cannot operate in a totally unregulated free market. They depend on the U.S. government (through the FDIC) to insure bank deposits, the SIPC to insure securities brokerage accounts, and the SEC to enforce disclosure of important information and make sure that exchanges are operated fairly, that the courts enforce purchase contracts, and so on.

As a society, we put rules in place to regulate what is and isn't allowed. Those rules shape what we call the market. When so-called free market advocates talk about letting the market make decisions, what they really mean is letting the existing rules play out. Unsurprisingly, this inevitably means that the people who are already doing well under the current system will continue to do well, while the people who are suffering continue to suffer.

If it were true that the market as currently structured can naturally take care of everything, it would have done so already. The idea that things will magically change on their own without any actual structural change is make-believe, no more defensible than believing Santa Claus and the Tooth Fairy will come and give every minimum-wage worker a raise themselves. It's not going to happen, and anyone telling you otherwise is insulting your intelligence. We've let the market work for decades, and workers aren't doing any better. If anything, they're doing worse.

In the immediate aftermath of the COVID-19 pandemic, wages for low-wage workers rose slightly as the labor market tightened.[14] But it didn't last. Instead of ushering in a new era of worker empowerment, those few years of higher-than-average wage gains look more and more like a momentary blip. Wage growth slowed in 2023, barely keeping pace with inflation.[15] Even worse, some companies are going so far as to roll back previous wage increases. This is what happens when the game is rigged against workers. Even when workers make minor gains, it's only a matter of time before corporations reassert themselves. We can't assume that the market will fix things or be fair. The only way to protect workers at the margin is for the government to mandate it.

Myth #6: An increase in the minimum wage will drive costs up, so everyone ends up paying more.

Right-wing economists have long predicted that increasing the minimum wage will lead to inflation as more people have more money to spend. This argument essentially claims that society should impose austerity upon one part of the population so that the other part of the population can have more. But evidence from previous federal minimum-wage increases, as well as dozens of more recent state-level increases, show that's not the case.[16] Once again, *we don't have to guess what happens when we raise the minimum wage.* We know what happens because we've done it many times before. And each time, prices haven't risen at all.

Congress last voted to raise the minimum wage in 2007. It increased that year from $5.15 an hour to $5.85, to $6.55 in 2008, and finally to $7.25 in 2009.[17] If the critics were right, inflation would have been abnormally high in those years and the years soon after. But it wasn't.

In the five years before Congress voted to raise the minimum wage, inflation averaged about 2.6 percent each year. In the three years during which the minimum wage was steadily increasing, inflation averaged about 2.1 percent annually.[18] In the five years after, prices rose by just 2 percent per year. Instead of seeing prices increase more rapidly, the country saw inflation slow after the minimum wage was increased. The evidence doesn't show any definitive correlation either way between price changes and higher minimum wages—instead, it suggests that they may not be connected at all.

For those who say that the current demands of minimum-wage advocates would somehow be different, there are more recent examples. While inflation became a meaningful problem in 2021 and 2022, there was basically no connection between a state's minimum wage and the amount of inflation it was facing.[19] Each of the states with at least a $15 minimum wage (California, Connecticut, Massachusetts, and Washington) had inflation levels roughly equal to, or slightly below, the national average. The two states with the highest levels of inflation, Colorado and Utah, sit at opposite ends of the spectrum. In 2022 Colorado had a minimum wage of $12.56, higher than most other states. But Utah faced the exact same problems with a minimum wage of just $7.25 per hour.

In most industries, wages simply aren't that large a percentage of the cost of doing business. Increasing wages for workers will cost companies more money, but it's often on a scale that the company can easily afford to swallow without passing increases on to consumers. Even in the most labor-intensive industries like fast food, total labor costs (including salaries for management and executives) barely account for one-third of total expenses.[20] In most other industries, that number is much lower. As United Auto Workers union president Shawn Fain said in 2023 when his union was striking against the Big Three automakers (General Motors, Stellantis, and Ford), "The cost of labor for a vehicle is 5% of the vehicle. They could double our wages and not raise the prices of vehicles, and they would still make billions of dollars."[21]

Myth #7: Minimum-wage workers don't earn more because their labor isn't worth more.

There is no such thing as a worthless job (except perhaps for lobbyists fighting against raising the minimum wage). Corporate America is brutally efficient, and the fat is constantly being cut. Even the absolute lowest-level position is necessary for the proper functioning of the organization it's a part of—otherwise, that position wouldn't exist, or at least not for long. It matters little how entry-level or "low skill" a job is (or is perceived to be), there is someone in that role because it is essential.

Low-wage workers make more money for their employers than what they're paid; otherwise, they wouldn't have been hired. But because of significant power disparity between corporations and employees when it comes to negotiating pay, workers are paid at below-market value and are often treated as if they're disposable. Relative negotiating power, not actual value, is what determines wages.

When you consider how much worker productivity has increased over time, the stagnation of the federal minimum wage becomes even more appalling. American workers have become significantly more productive over time, with each worker producing more widgets and serving more customers today than ever before. Between 1979 and 2020, net productivity for American workers increased by 61.8 percent.[22] While they're doing more and creating more value for their employers, workers in America haven't seen their increased productivity reflected in their pay. In that same time frame, when adjusted for inflation, average hourly wages have increased by only 17.5 percent. At the bottom, things are even worse—when adjusted for inflation, the federal minimum wage has *decreased* by 39 percent since 1979.[23] If the amount of value created is all that matters, today's low-wage workers would be solidly middle class. But much of the extra production of American workers has instead gone to the highest wage earners and equity investors.

Things weren't always this bad for workers. Up until the mid-1970s, the minimum wage kept up with increases in productivity.[24] As workers produced more value for their employers, they were paid more. That's supposed to be an essential part of the social contract of capitalism. But in the 1970s a gap started forming, and really exploded during the Reagan administration, as workers became more productive while the minimum wage stayed flat. Instead of paying workers according to the value they produced, employers began to pocket more and more of the yield of their employees' labor, increasing profits while keeping wages low. In more recent decades, that gap has only continued to grow. We've said it before and we'll say it again: if the minimum wage had kept pace with both inflation and productivity gains since 1968, it would be nearly $26 an hour.

Myth #8: Eliminating the tipped minimum wage (where tipped workers earn a lower minimum wage plus tips) means people won't tip and thus tipped workers will earn less.

The Fair Labor Standards Act specifies that if a worker makes the minimum wage, after counting tips, then that is a sufficient legal income. In fact, the law states that workers must receive either $2.13 per hour plus all tips OR the minimum wage of $7.25 per hour, whichever of the two amounts is greater. The employer is thus allowed to include tips when calculating whether they meet their obligation to pay minimum wage. This is called "tip credit."

There are seven states (Alaska, California, Minnesota, Montana, Nevada, Oregon, and Washington) with no tip credit, with tipped workers earning at least the standard minimum wage plus tips. Tipped workers in each of those states generally earn more than their counterparts in states that allow the employer to use the tip credit. The poverty rate for tipped workers in industries that heavily rely on tips in the other forty-three states is 14.8 percent, compared with just 11 percent in the seven states with "One Fair Wage." [25]

This tracks with findings that indicate people don't tend to tip less just because they're in a state that has abolished the subminimum tipped wage. People tip about the same no matter what the base wage for tipped workers is in their state, making an increase to the subminimum tipped wage an almost universal net positive for workers. [26] Evidence shows that waiters and bartenders earn on average about 20 percent

The Seven States Where Minimum Wage Workers Get Tips in Addition

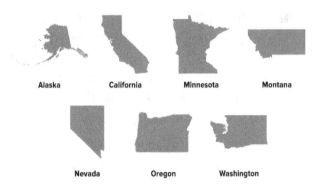

SOURCE: Department of Labor, Minimum Wage for Tipped Employees https://www.dol.gov/agencies/whd/state/minimum-wage/tipped

more, after tips, in states where tipped workers must be paid the full minimum wage plus tips.

This makes sense if you take the perspective of a typical restaurant customer rather than that of a cherry-picked economist. Changing the law to give workers a more stable base wage doesn't change our attitudes about what is a reasonable amount to tip. When was the last time you went out to eat and asked your server what they made in income before tips, or looked up what your state's tipped minimum wage was when deciding whether to tip 15 or 20 percent? It's just not something on most people's radar.

Another unfounded claim suggests that requiring restaurants to pay their servers enough that they don't need to rely on tips will cause the entire industry to fold. If there were any evidence that eliminating the subminimum tipped wage would lower the number of restaurant jobs available, we would see it in the seven states that don't have a subminimum tipped wage. But we don't.

Studies show that restaurant industry growth in those seven states is strong—so strong, in fact, that job growth in the restaurant industry and restaurant sales per capita in those states are higher than the national average. There's an argument, based on the data, that the restaurant industry does *better* in states where tipped workers make the standard minimum wage.

The Dumb, the Bad, and the Criminal

George Zimmer is the founder of Men's Wearhouse, and founder and CEO of Generation Tux.

"You're going to like the way you look. I guarantee it."

If you owned a TV at any point during the 1980s, '90s, or 2000s, you probably heard my famous slogan at least a few times. Men's Wearhouse, the company I founded in 1973, invested in television advertising for decades, and unlike most other CEOs of the time, I decided that consumers deserved to hear directly from me. No frills, no actors, no celebrity spokespeople in our ads—just me promising a quality product for an affordable price

It didn't take long for my face and my voice to become inextricably linked with Men's Wearhouse's public image. Other CEOs would have balked at putting their own personal reputation on the line for their business, but for me it was easy. I had absolute confidence that customers at Men's Wearhouse were going to be happy with their experience, because I had absolute confidence in the thousands of people we employed across the country.

From the very beginning when we had just a single store in Houston, I knew that my company was only going to be successful if the people working for it were fully bought in. I tried to build a company culture that truly valued every single employee, and showed them that they were valued not just through pizza parties, but through good pay. At Men's Wearhouse, everyone was paid fairly, and most employees were given additional financial incentives on top of their standard pay to keep them invested in their work. Within a few years of opening, we compensated employees 3 percent of what they sold. In the 1980s, we started an Employee Stock Ownership Plan, or ESOP, which offered company stock to employees on top of their normal salaries.

By spreading the company's stock around broadly, we gave thousands of employees a real financial interest in the company's success, and a chance to build wealth. I know of at least one worker who joined the company in the 1980s and left around 2010, and had close to a million dollars from the ESOP when he retired.

These kinds of financial rewards for employees were part of the reason the company was successful for so long, but they weren't always popular with my peers. It wasn't easy to keep a company as large as Men's Wearhouse focused on treating its employees with dignity and respect, especially after we went public in the early 1990s.

It's scary how incentives change when Wall Street gets involved. As CEO I made sixty-four quarterly calls and I developed quite a lot of experience with talking to Wall Street, and let me tell you—they see a financial quarter as "middle term," and a year out is about as far as they look into the future. It's no wonder their brand of capitalism is undercutting the long-term health of so many companies. It's not that their plans are wrong, it's that they don't even exist.

We were losing our way and I tried to correct our course, but in the end, I was ousted by other people at the company who wanted to go in a different direction. After twenty years as a public company, they felt like they'd put up with my liberal BS for long enough and they were going to move on. It only took them seven years to drive the company into bankruptcy.

Since then, I've stayed in the suit game, but moved out of the physical space and into the virtual one. I founded Generation Tux, an online suit and tuxedo rental platform, in 2014 and never looked back. And wouldn't you know it, even in the modern, decentralized, online era, paying your workers well and treating them with dignity pays off.

Generation Tux has a distribution center in Louisville, Kentucky, and, like many similar businesses, we had some trouble adequately staffing up after the initial COVID-19 wave in 2020. We were paying an entry-level wage of $11.50, but that wasn't cutting it. I decided we needed to make it $13 per hour.

Going from $11.50 to $13 is a modest increase. But it made a world of difference, both for company culture and for our turnover numbers. This is why it's so frustrating to see other executives make the same mistake over and over again. It doesn't cost that much to build trust and buy-in with your employees. It's not that hard or that expensive. All it takes is a genuine effort to make sure employees can trust that the company has their back. Do that, and your business will be better off.

The classic criticism deployed by some business figures is that if workers are paid more, then companies will collapse. But if your business can only afford to exist by paying your employees starvation wages, perhaps your business does not deserve to exist. Plenty of competent business owners and executives find ways to not just survive while paying their workers a decent wage, but thrive using that strategy. The businesses that will suffer from a higher minimum wage are ones that probably do not deserve to exist in the first place.

Small businesses are the heart of the American economy and the ultimate culmination of many an American dream, but again, the right to run a small business isn't absolute. The ability to run a profitable business does not supersede the right of workers to earn a decent wage. If a small business owner can make things work within the very reasonable requirements that we put on them, then that is fantastic. If they can't make it work, then maybe business ownership isn't right for them.

Currently, the American government is subsidizing bad business practices. By setting the minimum wage below what it materially costs to live in the United States, and providing economic support to the very workers who would otherwise be unable to survive, the taxpayers subsidize business owners who refuse to pay their workers adequately. American taxpayers are keeping exploitative businesses afloat. Even worse, other, more responsible businesses are subsidizing their competitors through the taxes that they pay. The government sets the rules of the economy, and it has established an operating environment that makes it easier for incompetent and greedy business owners to succeed while making things more expensive for everyone else.

The Dumb

Every time there's a new push by activists and progressive politicians to raise the minimum wage, it's met almost immediately by a rotating cast of CEOs, billionaires, and finance "experts" who claim that paying workers more will destroy businesses, cause massive layoffs, and hurt the economy.

Some of them might honestly believe that, but a lot of them are just posturing. They're not trying to save low-wage jobs and boost the economy; they're trying to protect broken business models and hoard short-term profits. They think that paying workers more will mean less money for them and their peers. They fight against a fair minimum wage not out of altruism, but out of short-term greed.

Most decisions made by business leaders are motivated by profit. But this approach to limiting wages is so shortsighted that they're making themselves poorer and the economy weaker. Paying workers as little as possible may keep expenses down, but for most businesses, worker pay is a relatively small percentage of total costs. It doesn't matter how little a company is able to pay its workforce if it isn't making money, and the only way a company can make money is if its customers have enough money to spend on whatever that company is selling.

It's like the classic 1972 Stanford marshmallow experiment

on children. The child has a choice: take one marshmallow now, or wait and get two marshmallows after a few minutes. Some have the willpower to wait for the reward of more marshmallows later. Others lack impulse control or foresight and scarf down the single marshmallow immediately. Too many of today's business leaders fail the marshmallow test. They are focused on consuming as much as they can as quickly as they can, even if it means they finish with less.

The Bad

There's a crime wave happening in America. Businesses in virtually every city across the country are facing the same problem, plagued by lawlessness that the police are helpless to stop. It's a sad sign of the times that a few small groups of people with no regard for decency are taking advantage of lax enforcement to collectively steal billions of dollars at retail establishments, restaurants, and other businesses that serve the community.

No, this is not about the shoplifting epidemic that many retailers complain about. This is about wage theft.

Every year in the United States, employers steal somewhere around $50 billion in wages from their employees.[1] That's more than three times the estimated $14.7 billion lost to shoplifting each year, and more than twice the value of all the burglaries, car thefts, and robberies that occur each year *combined*. Compared with the executives who illegally underpay their employees, professional shoplifters are amateurs.

SOURCE: AFL-CIO, Company Pay Ratios https://aflcio.org/paywatch/company-pay-ratios

Wage theft is insidious and quiet, a crime of omission rather than action. It's easy to miss, but these quiet crimes, adding up to thousands of cases each day, constitute the most widespread and impactful form of theft in the United States. No one is going to be televising videos on the local news of a minimum-wage employee working overtime without pay, or a restaurant owner pocketing half of a server's tips. Over 4.5 million workers face wage theft each year in the United States, and of those, more than 300,000 drop below the poverty line because they're underpaid by their employers.[2]

Most often committed against low-wage workers (those least able to afford it), wage theft is any instance where an employer pays a worker less money than they are legally entitled to. Sometimes it's obvious, such as when unscrupulous construction contractors skip paying their undocumented immigrant workers because they know that they will never engage the government to report them. Most of the time it is nearly invisible—some workers might not even know that they are being ripped off. It can be something as small as not providing legally mandated breaks or taking deductions from a worker's paycheck for mistakes on the job. Workers might also be illegally classified as independent contractors, who are exempt from minimum-wage laws. A pizza delivery driver who is an employee is legally required to make the minimum wage. A delivery driver who is a contractor can be paid per delivery, with no pay whatsoever if there happen to be no deliveries during his shift.

Wage theft is particularly bad in industries where wage laws are already compromised. In the restaurant industry, for instance, some establishments take a cut of their servers' tips, a practice that is illegal. On the flip side, when those tips aren't coming in, many employers fail to pay their workers enough to ensure they earn at least the minimum wage. Tipped employees can be paid as low as $2.13 per hour but they are supposed to earn at least $7.25 per hour. If there aren't enough tips in a shift to make up for that gap, the employer is legally required to cover the difference. They rarely do. In a study of full-service restaurants, the Department of Labor found that a whopping 84 percent had committed some form of wage theft.[3]

Workers in different states have vastly different resources when it comes to fighting against wage theft. The federal

Department of Labor will take cases anywhere, but it's stretched so thin that workers cannot rely on the federal government for support. Instead, they're forced to turn to their state governments. In blue states, this option may be fine. In a small number of states, like New Jersey, if the state labor department has determined that a company has committed a wage theft violation and also has failed to pay the subsequent fine, it will threaten to shut down the firm and suspend its business license.[4] Workers in big cities in these states, like New York or Los Angeles, have even more options. They can submit complaints to their city government as well.

Workers in red states, however, are forced to deal with the consequences of the intimate relationship between Republican lawmakers and business. They have weak worker-protection laws, and their state departments of labor are typically underfunded. In some states, like Alabama or Florida, there is no way for workers to file a state-level wage theft claim at all.

Overtime

One of the most common forms of wage theft is failing to pay for overtime. Employers might expect workers to work late every day to help clean up after their scheduled shift, while only paying them for the hours they "officially" worked. That adds up to dozens of hours of free work a year. They might misclassify an employee as a manager and offer them a salary instead of an hourly wage in order to illegally avoid paying for the extra hours.

Overtime pay, typically 150 percent of an employee's normal pay starting at the forty-first hour of their workweek, used to be the norm in America. If you worked more than forty hours a week, you made more money per hour than normal. As time has passed, however, overtime pay has become rarer, even as employees work longer hours, because corporations have started gaming the system. About 18 million salaried employees in America work for more than fifty hours a week, and a significant number of them receive no overtime pay whatsoever.[5]

Many employers try to claim that their employees are "managers" and therefore exempt from overtime. In its definition of "manager," the government has added the criterion of earning a salary above a certain threshold. That income threshold used to be relatively high, and overtime pay was common. In 1975, more than 60 percent of full-time salaried employees qualified for overtime pay.[6] Since then, the interpretation of what is considered "exempt" loosened, and the income threshold failed to keep pace with inflation. Today, just 15 percent of salaried employees qualify for overtime.[7]

Consider that if the law had kept pace with inflation and rising wages, the threshold would be more than double what it is today. Pegging the number to the rough percentage of the workforce it covered in the 1970s, a threshold that would cover 55 percent of full-time salaried workers in the United States. would need to be more than $82,500.[8]

Clearly, the most important solution to this problem is for the president or Congress to raise the overtime threshold to a

Federal Policy can Guarantee
Overtime Rights for more Workers

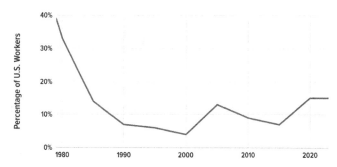

SOURCES: Center of American Progress, *America's Incredible Shrinking Overtime Rights Need an Update*, https://www.americanprogress.org/article/americans-incredible-shrinking -overtime-rights-need-an-update/
Economic Policy Institute, *More than eight million workers will be left behind by the Trump overtime proposal*, https://www.epi.org/publication/trump-overtime-proposal-april-update
Senator Sherrod Brown, Brown Introduces Bill To Make Millions of American Workers Eligible for Overtime Pay, https://www.brown.senate.gov/newsroom/press/release/sherrod-brown -introduces-bill-millions-american-workers-eligible-overtime-pay
The White House President Barack Obama, *FACT SHEET: Growing Middle Class Paychecks and Helping Working Families Get Ahead By Expanding Overtime Pay*, https://obamawhitehouse .archives.gov/the-press-office/2016/05/17/fact-sheet-growing-middle-class-paychecks-and -helping-working-families-0

more appropriate level. But we also need better enforcement of our current laws. Much of corporate America has figured out that there's virtually no penalty for gaming the system and misclassifying workers as "managers" if their incomes are just above the threshold.

A study by economists at Harvard University and the University of Texas at Dallas found that there is an epidemic of jobs that have salaries just barely over the $35,568 threshold, along with misleading titles that imply managerial duties but involve no actual management whatsoever.[9] From 2010 to 2019, the number of jobs mislabeled as managerial increased by 485 percent, with absurd examples ranging from listing a barber as a "grooming manager" to listing a restaurant hostess as a "guest experience leader." By paying these workers $36,000 or more and describing them as managers, corporations avoid thousands of dollars in overtime pay, averaging out to savings of almost 14 percent per "manager." In some cases, these managers end up being paid *less* per hour than they were before their "promotion," because they're required to work more hours without compensation.

To be clear, this is illegal. Classifying a worker as a manager when they do not actually manage, for the express purpose of not paying overtime, is against the law. But it's almost never enforced, which is why many corporations do it.

The Criminal

Many workers don't fully know their rights. A "manager" might not know that they're being taken advantage of by not being paid overtime. A cashier forced to work through lunch might not know that they're legally required to be given a lunch break. A worker might think it's unfair that their pay is docked for making a mistake at work, but they don't know it's illegal. Without proper awareness and education, it's challenging for workers to know what counts as their employer being demanding versus what crosses the line into illegal wage theft.

Even when workers know that their wages are being stolen, they have few options to resolve their problem. There is always a power dynamic in any workplace. Challenging your boss or your company could result in having your shifts cut or being fired outright. That's obviously a labor law violation, but it's hardly a stretch to think that an employer willing to bend the law to steal from their employees wouldn't also be willing to fire an employee for complaining about it.

This is the big problem with wage theft violations—the more precarious the position a worker is in, the less likely they are to be able to take a stand. Losing a few dozen dollars every paycheck is bad if you're struggling, but it's a disaster to lose your job entirely. Hence these crimes disproportionately affect low-wage workers. People earning hundreds of thousands of dollars a year have options that people earning $20,000 a year don't. They must keep working, even when they know they're getting exploited, because the alternative is they won't be able to pay their bills.

For immigrants, the dangers are even greater. Legal immigrants often have their residency status tied to their job, and losing it would mean losing their ability to legally reside in the United States. Undocumented immigrants are even more vulnerable. The fact that unscrupulous employers know that undocumented immigrants will almost never reach out to the government for help makes them much more susceptible to wage theft and labor violations.

For those intrepid workers who choose to take a chance and make a legal claim with the government, the likelihood of success is low. Both the federal Department of Labor (DOL) and its state counterparts are underfunded and overloaded with claims. There are barely more than a thousand investigators in the DOL's Wage and Hour Division tasked with covering a workforce that contains more than 150 million workers. That's so few that the National Employment Law Project estimates that at current capacity, the DOL has the ability to recover less than 4 percent of wages stolen by employers.[10]

Even when a case is taken on, the median resolution time for cases is six months (if it's resolved at all), with many taking more than a year.[11] And if you can imagine that complaining at your workplace might get you fired, it's logical to think that bringing an official wage theft complaint to the local authorities would make your firing even more likely. Submitting these claims is incredibly risky for workers.

A public records request by CBS News found that out of over 650,000 wage theft complaints, state agencies ruled in favor of the worker only about half the time.[12] Even when they win, many workers still never receive the money they're legally entitled to. In over a third of the cases where workers won, there is no record of those workers receiving the money they were owed, an amount that totaled over a billion dollars.

Some businesses, particularly ones that consistently steal from their employees, will use a collection of shell companies to avoid the legal consequences of their actions. If ABC Corporation owes its former employees $500,000 in back pay, it's often relatively simple for the owners to dissolve ABC Corp. and reconstitute it as DEF Corp. That doesn't automatically erase the previous business's legal liabilities, but it does make it harder for the DOL to enforce judgments against it. Such businesses will slip through the cracks and will never have to pay back the wages they stole.

Masking a company via shells isn't the only trick employers use to avoid accountability for wage theft. They also increasingly force low-wage workers to sign employment contracts that prevent them from ever participating in a class-action lawsuit over wage theft. Instead, all wage complaints are limited to either forced arbitration—a notoriously pro-business process with little upside for complainants—or overburdened government agencies. Since government investigators are so overloaded with claims, one of the more common ways for workers to reclaim stolen wages is to rely on private attorneys running class-action lawsuits. Embarrassingly, more money is often recovered by private lawyers and class-action lawsuits than by federal and state agencies combined.[13] Being locked out of this option via employment contracts, as is the case for more than 17 million workers making less than $13 an hour, makes it much less likely workers will ever see justice.[14]

Getting Away with Wage Theft

Share of Oregon Bureau of Labor and Industries
Monetary Findings Recovered from Employers

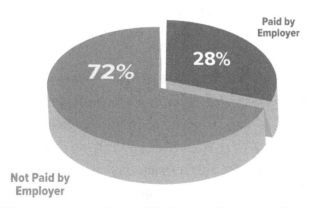

SOURCE: Oregon Center for Public Policy (OCPP) Analysis of Oregon Burea of Labor and Industries data of wage claims filed July 2010 to June 2013, https://www.ocpp.org/media/uploads/images/2015/wagetheftrecoveryMediumpng

Punish the Executives

Wage theft is a crime, and a particularly cruel one at that. It is perpetrated by some of the richest and most powerful corporations in American society, and targets some of its most vulnerable people. Someone making $25,000 a year cannot afford to go without $1,000 in wages. Someone living paycheck to paycheck cannot afford to lose that paycheck.

The difference between robbing a bank and skimming wages from a paycheck is that one will earn you a criminal conviction, while the other is treated as a purely statutory matter with relatively few penalties. If a shoplifter steals more than $2,500 in merchandise, he may be hit with felony charges. If a corporate boss steals $2.5 million from his employees, his company might have to pay back that amount, plus another $2.5 million in extra penalties. The executive himself will have to pay nothing and face no criminal charges. The implicit message the government sends is clear: if you're vulnerable and poor and steal from the rich, you can go to jail, but if you're rich and powerful and you steal from the poor, you can get away with it.

The felony theft threshold—the dollar value at which a theft elevates from a misdemeanor to a felony—is just a few hundred dollars in most states. Yet many businesses steal millions of dollars from their employees and face no charges. If the same standards were used for wage theft as they were for standard felony theft, more than a quarter of the 650,000 cases analyzed by CBS could have been charged as felonies.[15]

This double standard must change. The way to stop

companies and executives from stealing from employees is stricter enforcement and criminal charges levied against the people who willfully commit crimes. Until then, for many, the rewards of grifting from workers are going to be much greater than the costs of getting caught.

Some states, like Minnesota, New Jersey, and Illinois, passed laws along those lines, making wage theft a crime punishable by jail time.[16] But even in those states, enforcement is rare (or literally never, as is the case in New Jersey as of this writing). Prosecutors seem to have little interest in pursuing bad actors. Even after all the demonstrated cases of wage theft, only a handful of business owners have ever been prosecuted.

An Added Value

As the lives of CEOs, senior executives, and political leaders have become more detached from the lived experience of ordinary workers, something troubling is happening. Increasingly, they seem to treat workers less like people and more like costs. Executives often spend more time working with their peers than with their employees and teams. Mix in the growing "cult of the heroic CEO" in modern America, and you end up with lower-level managers who often miss the fact that their employees are in the same economic class as they are.

Every employee adds value to many lives. Whether they are delivery drivers, doormen (or -women), nannies, housekeepers, or some other kind of worker, the labor they perform contributes to society. But as the gross differences in pay between executives and entry-level workers has exploded, employees are treated less like equals and more like inanimate parts of a machine. That's why if we aim to fix the system, it's important for business leaders to take a different approach to valuing the contributions, and the humanity, of each of their workers.

Leading a corporation means constantly making thousands of large and small decisions about what kind of company you want to create. Do you value your employees and invest in them to ensure that they are supported and appreciated? Or do you treat them like interchangeable parts, whose principal element is cost?

If you're looking for two corporations that have come up with radically different answers to those questions, just look at the two largest employers in America: Walmart and Amazon. Both faced criticism over the years for the way their business practices have exploited low-wage workers. But in the last decade, as Amazon has doubled down on treating workers more like a necessary evil, Walmart has become the poster child for a corporation dedicated to treating its employees with dignity and respect.

Walmart

Walmart revolutionized retail by focusing on relentless cost reduction at every level of the company. As it expanded throughout the country and gobbled up markets from department stores and small businesses, the business juggernaut seemed unstoppable. It optimized for lowering costs for consumers, cost of supply, and running a lean staffing model—built around an army of minimum-wage workers. Through its success and scale, Walmart became one of the largest employers in its markets and locked in low wages for entire communities. Along the way it became Public Enemy No. 1 for the labor movement.

Although this model produced decades of explosive growth, problems emerged. Negative publicity damaged the company's brand, and labor groups and consumers were willing to pay extra to shop elsewhere in the fallout. Walmart faced growing rates of lost or stolen inventory. Walmart's minimum-wage workers had neither the expertise nor the motivation to continue to perform. If you also took into account turnover rates as high as 200 percent in some stores, Walmart's low wages, once considered by the company to be a competitive edge, began to appear more like a liability.

Walmart CEO Doug McMillon led Walmart's board in a different direction: it started to invest in its team. The company raised its base wage from just $7.25 an hour in 2015 all the way to $13 an hour by 2023, and focused on empowering low-wage employees to learn and grow within the company. Walmart embraced promotion from within. Increasingly, it improved the opportunities for its millions of workers to develop additional skills that helped them advance their careers through Walmart's worker academies. About 2.5 million employees have completed at least one course, learning new skills in areas from customer service to e-commerce.[1] Walmart promotes more than five hundred associates every single day, and 75 percent of managers in the company's U.S. stores started as hourly employees, a rarity in the corporate world.[2] In fact,

McMillon himself started at Walmart as an hourly employee as a teenager. He rejoined Walmart just two years out of college, starting as a buyer in charge of ordering fishing tackle for the company, and worked his way up through the ranks.

Walmart also made a concerted effort to consolidate (and support) its workforce by relying more on full-time employees, rather than part-timers. Instead of keeping its workers part-time to reduce benefits and wages, as many retailers do, Walmart concluded that investing in expanding full-time work would create a stronger workforce and company, and that the benefits would easily outweigh the additional costs. In 2016, about 50 percent of the company's workforce worked full-time. In 2022, that number passed two-thirds.[3]

Overall, 87 percent of full-time Walmart employees say they "really love" their jobs, and 88 percent "would definitely recommend" the company to someone looking for a job.[4] That's great for the workers, and great for Walmart. The decision to pay workers fairly was a moral one—McMillon invested in his team because he thought it was the right thing to do—but it was a sound business decision as well. Few companies in the United States are more focused on costs than Walmart. Its executives made the decision to treat their associates better not just to do the right thing, but because they understood that it would improve their business.

They were right. Despite Amazon's incredible success in the last decade, Walmart has comfortably maintained its spot as the company with the highest revenue in the United States. It took in about $100 billion more revenue than the second-largest company in 2015, ExxonMobil, and it takes in about

$100 billion more than Amazon, the current No. 2.[5] On the investor side, from October 2015 to August 2023, Walmart's stock price rose by 276 percent. The S&P 500, by comparison, rose just 223 percent over that same period. Anyone who bet on Walmart to succeed because of its decision to invest in its workers would have made quite a bit of money in the last eight years.

Amazon

In contrast to Walmart, Amazon, the second-largest corporation in the United States, has unabashedly chosen to prioritize efficiency over workers to a ruthless degree.[6] Amazon has become the poster child for worker exploitation—what *not* to do as a corporation. A company that was once famous for revolutionizing e-commerce is now notorious for its poor treatment of workers.

Amazon's apparent contempt for its own workers seems to come from the top. Jeff Bezos has said he believes that hourly work should be relatively short-term, and that keeping low-wage workers around for a long time leads to "a march to mediocrity."[7] He reportedly believes that people are inherently unmotivated, and that retaining low-wage workers leads to a less-eager, less-productive, disgruntled workforce. Despite his claim that he wants to make Amazon "Earth's best employer," Jeff Bezos apparently views much of his workforce not as teammates, but as an adversarial force that needs to be dominated in order to produce results.[8]

Amazon drivers, for example, face borderline impossible quotas, needing to deliver anywhere from 170 to 375 packages in a single ten-hour shift.[9] UPS drivers, for context, deliver about 225 packages a day.[10] Think about the actual logistics of delivering 375 packages in just ten hours. That is 37.5 packages an hour, one package every ninety-six seconds. Add in travel time and traffic, and it becomes a hugely challenging task, forcing delivery drivers to go to extremes to stay on pace. Amazon offers breaks to its drivers, but because of the intense pressure to keep delivery rates high, drivers are often forced to skip those breaks.[11] One driver told *The Intercept*, "They give us 30 minutes of paid breaks, but you will not finish your work if you take it, no matter how fast you are."[12]

Drivers for Amazon delivery are asked to deliver up to 375 packages per 10-hour shift

SOURCE: *Business Insider*, Amazon delivery drivers say there's a 'giant war' between them and the company as they struggle to meet package quotas, https://www.businessinsider.com/amazon -drivers-interview-giant-war-between-them-and-company-packages-2021-7

Instead of taking lunch, drivers will eat while they drive, sandwich in one hand and steering wheel in the other. Instead of taking water breaks, they'll take a swig here and there as they're hopping in and out of the van. And yes, instead of taking fifteen minutes to stop and find a bathroom and fall ten packages behind schedule, many drivers will instead pee in empty bottles in their vans.[13]

In its warehouses, Amazon exerts a Big Brother–esque amount of control over its workers, with constant surveillance and ever-increasing demands for higher productivity. The company monitors every single minute its warehouse employees are working, and penalizes them harshly for any amount of "time off task," or TOT, in which the employee is not actively working.[14] Employees can be penalized for anything from talking to another employee, going to the wrong floor of a warehouse, or taking too many bathroom or water breaks.

Amazon's high expectations of its low-wage workers often come at a heavy price. In 2022, data from the Occupational Safety and Health Administration (OSHA) shows that Amazon reported 6.6 serious incidents for every 200,000 hours worked (the equivalent of one hundred employees working full-time for a year), giving each Amazon warehouse worker a 1 in 15 chance of being seriously injured in a given year.[15] That rate is more than twice the industry average of 3.2 incidents per 100 workers, making Amazon one of the most dangerous major warehouse employers in America.

Amazon's injury rate was so high in 2021 that there were

more injuries that caused employees to take time off work or be transferred to light duty within Amazon's warehouses than there were in *every other warehouse in America combined.* Amazon's 308 warehouses produced 24,945 serious injuries, while 4,184 non-Amazon warehouses combined to produce only 24,338.[16]

Both OSHA and many workers claim that Amazon's high injury rates are directly linked to the company's single-minded focus on speed at all costs. The "pace of work," as one OSHA report puts it, is largely responsible for the high prevalence of MSDs, or musculoskeletal disorders.[17]

Injuries at Amazon Warehouses are Far Above National Average

Injury rate per 100 full-time employees at U.S. warehouses in 2020

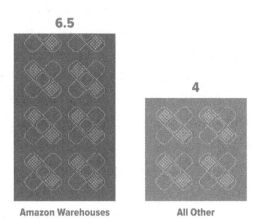

6.5

4

Amazon Warehouses   **All Other**

SOURCE: *Business Insider,* Amazon delivery drivers say there's a 'giant war' between them and the company as they struggle to meet package quotas, https://www.businessinsider.com/amazon -drivers-interview-giant-war-between-them-and-company-packages-2021-7

OSHA Fines

O n New Year's Eve 2022, Courtney Edwards, a thirty-four-year-old mother of three children, started working a shift on the ground crew at Montgomery Regional Airport in Alabama.[18] She would not make it home to celebrate the new year. Shortly after American Airlines Flight 3408 landed, as she made her way to the plane, Courtney was sucked into one of the aircraft's engines, and died. After an investigation, OSHA—the federal agency tasked with protecting worker safety—found that Piedmont Airlines, a subsidiary of American Airlines, was at fault. As a result of negligence resulting in the death of an employee, OSHA levied the maximum fine allowed under current labor law against the airline: $15,625.

American Airlines brought in $52.26 billion in revenue that year.[19] OSHA's fine ultimately accounted for 0.000029 percent of the airline's annual revenues. That's the equivalent of someone earning $70,000 a year and paying a fine of 2¢. American Airlines charges double that amount, $31,000, for a single round-trip, first-class ticket from New York to Tokyo. To American Airlines, $15,000 is so small a fine that it would be hard to notice.

We need new and significantly higher penalties for companies that illegally exploit their workers and put them at risk. Even the maximum fine for companies that commit "willful or repeated violations" is just $156,259 per violation.[20] That might discourage small businesses from breaking the law, but it's pocket change for big corporations. There's no incentive to avoid dangerous practices that put their workers at risk when the downside is a $15,000 fine.

Congress needs to strengthen OSHA's ability to pursue companies *that put their workers at risk. President Biden's Build Back Better plan featured a component, ultimately blocked by Senators Kyrsten Sinema and Joe Manchin in 2021, that would have given OSHA the ability to levy fines of up to $70,000 per serious violation, and up to $700,000 for willful or repeated violations.[21] Honestly, these are still small fees when compared with big corporate profits, but quadrupling the maximum fine is a good place to start.*

Consequences for Amazon

There's no denying that Amazon has become one of the largest companies in the world while treating its workers as a disposable cost. But as Walmart found out in the early 2000s, Amazon is discovering that kind of treatment has a long-term price. Amazon's treatment of its workers isn't just a problem for those workers—leaked internal research papers from within Amazon show that it's an expensive problem for the company, and one that might become a full-blown crisis within a few years.[22] According to the documents leaked in 2022, Amazon is running out of workers.

Industry experts have always known that Amazon had a higher-than-average turnover rate, but some of the numbers that have come out in recent years have been mind-blowingly bad. Only one-third of new hires last even just ninety days with the company, and of those two-thirds that leave, workers are twice as likely to leave by choice rather than being fired.[23] Also, the original plan wasn't for them to be temporary workers—Amazon's own data indicates that nine out of ten new employees say they want to stay for at least six months.[24]

Some of the company's own data paints an even darker picture. According to internal Amazon data, a shocking 3 percent of hourly employees leave Amazon every week.[25] That adds up to an annual turnover rate of over 150 percent. Amazon is essentially forced to replace its entire frontline workforce every single year. For context, similar companies typically aim for a turnover rate of 10 percent or less.[26] Within the warehouse industry that number is quite a bit higher, averaging around 43 percent, but even then, Amazon's numbers are 3.5 times the industry average.[27]

Amazon appears to treat most of its employees equally poorly. At Amazon, the problem starts with lowest-paid hourly workers but it does not end there. The lowest turnover rate for even the highest tier of Amazon employee is 69.5 percent, a group that includes managers of all levels, most of whom escape to better options when they realize that working at Amazon offers virtually no opportunities for internal advancement or promotions.[28] This is particularly true for hourly workers, according to David Niekerk, a former Amazon vice president of human relations, who said that the company "intentionally limited upward mobility for hourly workers."

Data shows that even those hourly workers who put in the time and effort to achieve positions of minor authority and responsibility are consistently overlooked for promotions in favor of fresh college graduates with little or no work experience. In 2021, only 4 percent of warehouse process assistants, a lower-level leadership role, were promoted to area managers, while 39 percent of open management positions were filled by new college graduates.[29]

High turnover rates have created an expensive problem for Amazon. The company estimates that its abnormally high attrition rate costs it $8 billion a year.[30] Even for a company as big as Amazon, that's a lot of cash—almost 25 percent of the $33.36 billion in net profits it reported in 2021.[31] And it's only getting worse.

In communities with Amazon warehouses, the company's reputation hurts its ability to hire. In some areas, particularly smaller towns, one out of every three workers has worked at the local warehouse. In those towns, people know how Amazon works its employees. And while almost 90 percent of Walmart workers would recommend working there to a friend or family member, many Amazon employees actively warn others away from the company.

Combine an enormous amount of employee turnover with a massive workforce of over a million workers, and you have some interesting math for Amazon's future. The company's own internal reports in 2021 said, "If we continue business as usual, Amazon will deplete the available labor supply in the U.S. network by 2024."[32] The company has churned though so many workers, and turned off so many others, that it faces the risk of not being able to hire enough workers. Amazon is rapidly turning to automation as a solution, aiming to increase warehouse productivity by 25 percent using robots.[33] At the end of the day, though, a lot of the work has to be done by humans.

Amazon has responded by raising its wages. It has now implemented a $15-per-hour minimum wage, an average starting wage of $19 per hour for frontline employees, higher pay in locations with tight labor markets, and hiring bonuses as high as $3,000.[34] These are all positive initiatives—of course, Amazon should pay its workers decently. But it also doesn't make up for a dysfunctional and exploitative workplace.

What Is a Job Worth?

There's a persistent belief in the United States in the efficiency of the market, and that workers are paid what they're worth. If you're paid a low wage, then perhaps you're not that valuable of a worker. If you're paid a high salary, you must be pretty amazing and those are your just deserts.

This is problematic, of course. Our capitalist markets are largely efficient—but not always. Especially for entry-level workers and low-wage employees, the expected laws of supply and demand do not apply.

In theory, workers could shop themselves around to various businesses bidding for talent, and eventually find a position that properly compensates them for the value they bring to the table. But the labor market is not a well-functioning market. For a market to function properly, it requires a lot of things that are missing in our current one—competition, transparency, and an ability for either the buyer or the seller to walk away from a bad deal. Without these, a fair and open market becomes what's known as an "inefficient" market, one where the price of things does not reflect their true value.

The current labor market is, indisputably, inefficient. The price of labor has very little relationship with how much value that labor provides and everything to do with which side of the inefficiency you're on. Decades of lackluster antitrust enforcement, declining union membership, and trickle-down economic policies have concentrated an enormous amount of power in the hands of a small number of corporate executives, and they have used that power to enrich themselves to an obscene degree.

On the other side, the average low-wage worker has precious little power to demand better pay, more comprehensive benefits, or improved working conditions. In any sort of negotiation, the side that is more willing to walk away from the table always holds more power. It's hard to imagine a larger imbalance in negotiating power than that between a multi-billion-dollar corporation and a minimum-wage worker who's a paycheck away from homelessness.

This is where government leadership comes in. While American workers might not have the power to properly negotiate on their own behalf in a vacuum, the American government has more than enough power to set the terms of that negotiation. The government uses labor laws, from minimum-wage laws to laws that mandate overtime pay and benefits, to create a framework that can help workers get a better deal. However, it has, unfortunately, done a terrible job of this in the last several decades.

What Makes a Job Essential?

The charade that low-wage workers aren't paid more because they're not valuable workers should have ended definitively in March 2020. With the global economy reeling from the outbreak of the COVID-19 pandemic and most of the American population in lockdown, ordinary life for most ground to a halt. As thousands died each day, people stayed inside for months, only leaving to pick up essentials and hurry back home. Millions stopped working, while millions more started to learn how to work remotely. Daily life changed to a previously unimaginable degree for everyone—except low-wage workers.

As the rest of us struggled with Zoom, millions of low-wage workers across America continued to go into work like normal because they worked in jobs deemed "essential." From grocery stores to trash dumps to chicken slaughterhouses, these newly minted "essential workers" had always kept the wheels of the American economy turning, performing the basic, unglamorous tasks that make daily life possible. With a booming economy, they were overlooked. But as the rest of the economy froze, it became clear just how critical it was for these people to continue showing up to work. There was no option for them to stop.

You can't stock grocery stores remotely. You can't pack up carryout orders over Zoom. The men and women who do the physical work to keep our economy moving and our population fed, sheltered, and healthy had no other option but to go into work, health risks and all.

Many essential workplaces, like farms and food preparation

1 in 4 Essential Workers are Having Difficulties Affording Basic Household Expenses

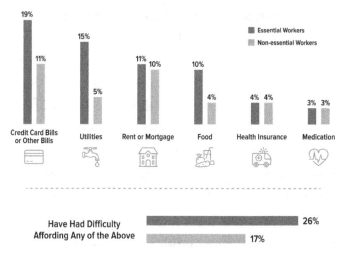

Have Had Difficulty Affording Any of the Above
26%
17%

NOTE: Essential workers are those who said they were required to work outside of their home.
SOURCE: KFF Health Tracking Poll (conducted April 15–20th, 2020).

facilities, had worksite conditions that made social distancing impossible. It certainly didn't help that some businesses treated low-wage workers as essentially disposable and refused to change protocols or provide enough protective gear to keep workers healthy. This disregard for the safety of workers ranged from saying one thing while doing another, to flat-out open disdain—one Tyson pork plant in Iowa actually had a "cash buy-in, winner-take-all betting pool for supervisors and managers to wager how many employees would test positive for COVID-19."[1] In their personal lives, low-wage workers were also more likely to live in housing with large groups of other people, and more likely to have underlying health conditions that put them at heightened risk.[2]

As a result of all these factors, low-wage workers faced significantly higher mortality rates during the pandemic. Workers in the food and agriculture sector experienced the worst. Their excess mortality rates were higher than workers in the health care industry, and they saw an increase in death rate almost twice that of the general population.[3] Line cooks, in particular, saw their mortality rate increase by 60 percent, almost three times the general population's increase of 22 percent.

During the crisis, the homebound general population realized the challenges of essential workers. They banged pots and pans together in the evening to thank essential workers and praised their work to journalists. Some low-wage workers received pay bumps or bonuses during the pandemic, but that appreciation was short-lived. Employers were required by law to offer two weeks of emergency paid sick or family leave, but this expired at the end of 2020.[4] Since then, we've returned to a situation where 21 percent of the nation's workforce has no paid sick leave.[5]

All of us want to move beyond the darker days of the pandemic and never think about it again. However, we should not lose that appreciation for those low-wage workers who took on greater sacrifices to serve the rest of us. They deserved better then, and they deserve better now. The pandemic showed us, without ambiguity or illusion, that many low-wage workers are some of the most important workers in our economy. Without them, we would be screwed. We cannot go back to the days of pretending these jobs or these people are superfluous. The workers in these jobs are essential, and they deserve to be paid like it.

All Work Has Value

If a job needs to be done, then the person doing it needs to be paid enough to live on. It is absurd that we have jobs that are important enough to be necessary for the function of a business or society, yet simultaneously *not* important enough to adequately pay the person doing it. There is no such thing as a job that is worth less than the cost of paying a fair wage.

Patricia Campos-Medina, the executive director of the Worker Institute at Cornell University, put it best: "All work is work and all work is dignified. All work produces value for our economy. Because professionals need to stop and buy a cup of coffee. And that worker should not be thought of as less value for selling you the coffee than for going into a corporate office."[6]

To be clear, not every low-wage worker is perfect. Employees are as diverse as the country. Some are highly motivated. Some are not. Some jobs are redundant, or about to be made obsolete by new equipment or automation. However, none of this can ever be assumed when pricing out entry-level worker wages. You must orchestrate compensation as though every single role in your company is important, because, as a practical matter—when you're hiring—they are.

Any changes to that plan can be addressed by competent management, whether through firing poor performers or eliminating positions that are no longer productive. That evolution of employees and roles within an organization is a natural part of business, and whether those changes excite or upset the team, it's healthy for an organization. Times change and organizations adapt. Not every job will exist forever, and often there's a point where a once-productive role doesn't make sense anymore to fill. But until the decision is made that a job isn't worth doing, the person doing it needs to be paid a decent wage.

Low-Skill Jobs Are Anything But

Every job requires a specific set of skills and abilities. The fact that the skills required for certain positions are not obtained through formal training and education does nothing to detract from the fact that even the most "low skill" jobs can demand high levels of skill and specific knowledge. The term "low skill" is really just another way to convey "low education requirement." It implies that the only professional skills that really matter are the ones that the richest Americans learn in college and develop in offices and white-collar jobs.

Many so-called low-skill workers, in fact, have similar abilities required to succeed in higher-paid positions. Being a good manager or a good HR professional requires organization, an ability to think on your feet, and great interpersonal competence. There are few workers with better "people skills" than restaurant servers, and balancing both the obvious and non-obvious needs for a dozen tables requires exceptional organizational and improvisational dexterity.

Some of the most capable workers in America are new immigrants making less than minimum wage for farmwork, harvesting crops with speed and precision for hours in incredibly demanding physical environments. One could hardly call that "low skill."

This might sound like semantics, but language matters. Language that diminishes the worth and ability of low-wage workers matters a lot. As journalist Annie Lowery puts it, "The term *low-skill* as we use it is often derogatory, a socially sanctioned slur Davos types casually lob at millions of American workers, disproportionately Black and Latino, immigrant, and low income."[7] Not only is the idea insulting to these communities, it's also used to undermine them from a policy perspective. The notion that low-wage work is unskilled work that anyone could do is used by some employers to justify underpaying their employees, and it's used by policymakers to justify ignoring the plight of low-wage workers.

The prevalence of the idea that people are only working in low-wage jobs exclusively because of a lack of skills is the reason that many workforce initiatives focus all too frequently on skills development. "Learn to code" was the key career advice in the mid-2000s. Yet today many of those "high skills" workers are threatened by artificial intelligence. Realistically, transforming most entry-level workers into software engineers is not a workable solution for most. It's certainly not the smartest path toward raising wages for millions of low-wage workers.

We are never going to have a purely white-collar economy. Entry-level and blue-collar jobs are integral parts of our economy. They need to be filled for our country to function. We spent the past few decades increasing the requirements to qualify for entering the white-collar workforce. Most candidates—regardless of their skills—need a college degree even to interview for higher-paid jobs.

During the Great Recession, an enormous amount of

attention was paid to the "skills gap."[8] The premise was that there were an increasing number of jobs that needed to be filled in the economy but that the workforce was incapable of filling them. The skills gap was sold as a *key* reason unemployment was so high. The structure of the economy had changed, went the argument made by everyone from the Obama White House to the Chamber of Commerce, and the workforce hadn't kept up. To shrink unemployment, we needed to embark on ambitious training programs to give millions of American workers new skills for a new economy.

Those training programs never materialized. The unemployment rate kept going down while the labor participation rate kept going up. Eventually, we reached a point of record low unemployment, all without any major change to the workforce's "skill" level.

It turns out the story of the skills gap was misleading. It distracted from the failure of a fiscal policy that was not adequately aggressive in boosting the economy out of its sluggish recovery. Research published by the American Economic Association discovered that the key reason there was a skills gap was that high unemployment had empowered businesses to be more picky.[9] As the labor market grew more competitive, businesses flexed their formal requirements for roles and were able to operate as before. Researchers found that "a 1 percentage point increase in the state unemployment rate is associated with a 0.6 percentage point increase in the fraction of employers requiring a bachelor's degree and a 0.8 percentage point increase in the fraction of employers requiring four or more years of experience." The jobs did not change—what changed was the hiring leverage of employers who could demand more qualifications and more education.

Skills are not the key driver of compensation—unregulated supply and demand is. Calling low-wage workers "low skill" puts the burden on them to gain "better" skills that will pay better, instead of addressing the broader systemic problems that make the skills they have—and the jobs they hold—inadequate. When we talk about skills and low-skill workers, we're distracted from the more important discussion about what really affects worker pay: leverage and bargaining power.

The Great Reshuffle

What happens when workers take back some power?

At times, it feels like the way our economy functions leads to an oversupply of despair and desperation. A one-sided labor market that favors management and undervalues low-wage workers, the failure of labor regulators to regulate, and the lack of a consistent social safety net combine to give a critical mass of American workers no option but to take whatever jobs they can, for wages that they can't afford.

When anything threatens that dynamic, such as the booming job market of 2021 and 2022, ruling powers push back. When the job market responds to demand signals where workers are able to negotiate wages and leave their job for better options, many businesses push back. For decades, business owners had been lulled into complacency by job markets in which they held the power and set all the terms.

With the unemployment rate dropping and workers feeling

more empowered to leave bad jobs, many businesses across the United States began to complain that "no one wants to work anymore." That line was repeated ad nauseam by business owners, political pundits, and conservative politicians who pretended to believe that the American work ethic was dying. But while "the Great Resignation" was in full swing, with a record 47.8 million workers quitting their jobs in 2021

and 50.5 million quitting in 2022, the American people hadn't stopped working—many just stopped working at jobs they could barely tolerate.[10]

It was easy to be misled by the very public and dramatic stories of workers quitting, such as the account of the staff of a Burger King in Lincoln, Nebraska, that all left mid-shift, leaving only a sign that read, "WE ALL QUIT, SORRY FOR THE INCONVENIENCE."[11] After all, few news outlets would follow up on what happened after all these workers quit, because the truth is more prosaic: many of them quietly got new, better, higher-paying jobs.

The "Great Resignation" might have made for a dramatic headline, but the "Great Reshuffle," as some have called it, is more accurate.[12] Many millions of workers who quit didn't exit the labor force; rather, they used their market power to move to positions with higher pay and better working conditions. In fact, the labor force participation rate—the percentage of the population that is either working or looking for work—grew during the Great Resignation.[13]

There was no shortage of people in America willing to work. There was a shortage, however, of workers willing to tolerate lousy pay and toxic working conditions. Sixty-three percent of workers who quit in 2021 cited low pay and no opportunities for advancement as reasons for leaving, and 57 percent said that they were leaving in part because they felt disrespected at work.[14] Those are good reasons to leave a job! The fact that workers feel empowered to leave situations where they feel underpaid and disrespected should be a sign that the economy is working well. It is not a good thing for workers to be trapped in terrible conditions indefinitely at the mercy of their employers.

Some in the business world, however, seemed uncomfortable that the demands of the market could work for employees as well as management. Bank of America, one of the largest and most powerful financial institutions in the United States, released an executive memo in the spring of 2022 (later leaked by *The Intercept*) saying it hoped that the unemployment rate would *increase* so that workers would have less leverage, expressing worry that a tight labor market would lead to rising wages across "virtually every industry, income and skill level." [15] To most Americans, this line of thinking is crazy. Low unemployment is good and rising wages are terrific.

It's important to point out that, despite complaints from some executives and business owners about higher wages and worker empowerment, from early 2020, just before the pandemic, corporate profits were over 700 billion annually.[16] Corporations were doing well, and so was the economy. There is no evidence that increased worker empowerment negatively affected the economy in any material way. The companies that did suffer had brought it on themselves by having a toxic work environment or underpaying their team, thus opening up the possibility of employees finding better-paying options elsewhere.

Based on the scale of increased corporate profits, business owners should have been thrilled with the state of the economy. The problem, however, is that many of the people in charge are deeply uncomfortable with worker empowerment. Hearing that low-wage workers, treated like cogs that keep the businesses running, were asking for more money, or leaving for other jobs, just does not conform with the way they see the world. So, they insisted that the economy must be suffering despite most indicators showing nothing but blue skies and sunshine.

Moral Superiority

Perhaps part of the reason that some people, from CEOs and managers to political leaders and voters, have little interest in helping low-wage workers is that they consider the working poor to be not just an economic class, but moral failures in some way. The implicit bias seems to be that if someone is part of the working poor, then it must be their fault.

For the well-off person, it might be comforting to think that the reason someone is poor and the well-off person is not is because the well-off person and their family did something right while the poor person did something wrong; or that somehow that the well-off person made the right choices in their life and the working poor made the wrong ones. That's not how society works. Environment, status, good and bad fortune equally tip the scale of opportunity. Someone born into a wealthy family is exponentially more likely to end up rich than someone born into a poor one. Personal decisions obviously make a difference, but no matter how hard you try, it's a lot harder to win a footrace when you start behind the pack, and in some cases off the track entirely.

Morris had dinner one night in the apartment of one of the wealthiest people in New York, who currently lives in the same apartment where he was born, in an apartment building that his grandfather bought roughly a century ago. Morris asked him what he thought about an article in that day's newspaper about some people living in a dreadful homeless shelter, with a picture of an eleven-year-old girl in the shelter prominently displayed on the front page. He said that people need to take responsibility for their decisions. This man is apparently taking full responsibility for his "decision" to be the grandson of a real estate magnate. Morris suggested that he didn't know what decisions an eleven-year-old girl might have made differently. The man corrected his response to say that parents must take responsibility for their decisions. Needless to say, he and Morris don't spend much time together anymore.

The willful blindness of the rich is everywhere. And it's no wonder. It is uncomfortable to accept that in a different set of circumstances, you could just as easily be the one unhoused. It forces us to reckon with their humanity in a way that we might not otherwise. And because that's hard to do, many people will instead look for ways to ignore or punish the poor for their "sins."

This isn't just idle social commentary—this subconscious idea that the poor are less virtuous than the rich is a major reason our society treats them so badly. At every turn, the poor are regarded as if they're doing something wrong, even if they're doing everything right and still struggling. It's why raising the minimum wage isn't a priority for many lawmakers; it's why many parts of our social safety net throw up obstacles to obtaining aid and assistance.

This warped worldview has tangible consequences for poor Americans, but it's also psychologically traumatizing. We hear it consistently from low-wage workers—one of the worst parts of being poor isn't the actual deprivation, it's the loss of dignity. To rely on charity and government assistance, to not be able to provide for your family, is, in the eyes of many, to concede that you have failed. Each of us wants to be able to stand on our own to provide for ourselves without having to ask others for help. But even when low-wage workers have full-time work (and often extra shifts beyond that) and are doing everything in their power to lift themselves out of the low-wage poverty trap, the ground is sinking below them. The game is rigged, and they're set up to lose from the start.

Let's be clear—needing help from others is not a moral failure. Relying on charity does not make you any less of a worthwhile person, or any less of a good father or mother. Losing

School Lunch Debt

Many school cafeterias don't require students to pay immediately for each of their meals. Instead, each student has an account with the cafeteria that either they or their parents will put money into to pay off meals as they come. When there's not enough money in their account, schools will still give that child a meal, but they'll have a negative balance in their account.

This isn't a big deal for families that can immediately top up their child's account, but for low-income families, school lunch debt can stack up, eventually leading to debt collection notices, public shaming, and schools barring children from receiving any more meals. Students with lunch debt are often given worse, "alternative" meals, such as a single peanut butter and jelly sandwich.[17] They can also be denied food altogether, sometimes for debt totals as low as $10. Without a meal, children are left to deal not just with hunger, but with shame. A student sitting in the cafeteria with no lunch is a clear, public, and humiliating signal to all the other students that he or she is poor.

Sometimes the shaming doesn't come from other children, but from the school itself. One Alabama school sent children with lunch debt home with a stamp on their hands that read, "I need lunch money."[18] Another school threw a child's lunch in the trash—on his birthday—because his parents owed $9.[19] One Pennsylvania school district threatened to put children into foster care if their parents couldn't pay their lunch debt.[20]

These are all despicable practices and would be out of line even if parents owed thousands of dollars. However, in many cases, we're talking about a few dollars at most. A 2023 survey showed that students around the country owed about $19 million in meal debt.[21] This is a small number in the grand scheme of spending on our schools and on nutrition assistance, yet it's been used to shame and embarrass thousands of small children. It would be cheap and easy to give a free meal to every single child in America's schools—so easy, in fact, that through special congressional action we did just that during the COVID-19 pandemic. But as with so many other significant anti-poverty victories during that time, we let the program expire.

a game that was rigged from the start does not make you a loser; it means the game was unfair. The only moral failing is that of the wealthy and powerful people who have deliberately designed our economic system to make themselves richer at the expense of working Americans. They are the ones who should be ashamed.

The Politics of Wages

Raising the minimum wage is one of the most popular issues in American politics. Most polls shows that a significant majority of voters, including most Republicans, agree that the federal minimum wage should be much higher.[1] You might think that this would make it a no-brainer for Congress to vote to raise the minimum wage. Unfortunately, Congress doesn't always legislate based on public opinion— it's much more concerned with the interests of the rich and powerful.

We live in a democracy, but in many ways, it feels more and more like an oligarchy. At the end of the day, money makes things happen in Washington. When rich people want the government to do something for them, they usually get their way, even when it comes at the expense of everyone else. In fact, research by Martin Gilens of Princeton and Benjamin Page of Northwestern found evidence that when it comes to policy change, the only opinions that matter are those of rich people and organized interest groups like the Chamber of Commerce.[2] What the public wants, in contrast, has virtually no influence on Congress. The only time the American people get policies that they truly want is when it coincides with what big business and rich Americans want.

This shouldn't come as much of a shock. Winning an election keeps getting titanically more expensive, and the rising costs of running for office keep pushing members of Congress to focus more and more of their time on fundraising from big donors. The 2022 midterms cost a record $8.9 billion in total.[3] The average senator running that year raised more than $13.5 million, and the average House candidate raised $1.8 million. That big money has to come from somewhere, and members of Congress, on average, now spend at least half their time fundraising. Who do you think is willing and able to spend $5,000 to sit next to a senator during a fancy fundraiser? It's not the line cook at your local Denny's who earns $9 per hour. There might be a lot more low-wage workers than there are rich political donors in the United States, but those donors spend enormously more on campaign contributions and lobbying than poor workers.

Even if a senator or representative isn't consciously making the decision to prioritize the needs of the rich over everyone else, they're going to inevitably end up with a skewed view of the world when they spend almost all their time talking to rich people. This was illustrated clearly for us at a congressional

Average Persons' Policy Preferences

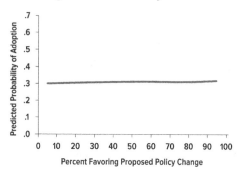

Economic Elites' Policy Preferences

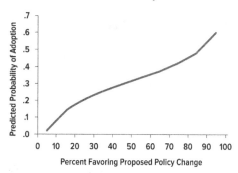

Interest Group Alignments

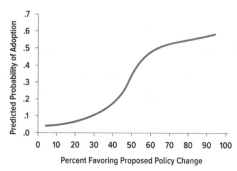

SOURCE: Martin Gilens and Benjamin I. Page, "Testing Theories of American Politics: Elites, Interest Groups, and Average Citizens," *Perspectives on Politics*, https://www.cambridge.org/core /journals/perspectives-on-politics/article/testing-theories-of-american-politics-elites-interest -groups-and-average-citizens/

fundraiser in New York that we both attended a few years ago. The candidate, a sitting member of Congress, said that he was happy to do fundraising because he got to spend time with "regular people." Mind you, we were standing in a high-rise penthouse in Manhattan, nowhere near this member's district, at a party that cost at least a thousand dollars per person to attend. The only "regular people" in that room were the ones serving us hors d'oeuvres. That's the mindset too many of members of Congress have.

Two Parties, One Problem

Here's the uncomfortable truth: the Republican Party is a lost cause on the minimum-wage issue, but Democrats haven't been much better.

Democrats in the House were able to pass a $15 minimum-wage bill in 2020, but eight of the fifty members of the Senate Democratic Caucus blocked that bill from becoming law in March 2021. It's easy (and logical in some ways) to blame Republicans for their opposition to paying workers more, but it is an undeniable fact that if every member of the Democratic caucus in Congress voted to raise the minimum wage, we would have a $15 minimum wage. The party leadership's unwillingness to enforce a hard line on this issue has allowed a few corporations and high-dollar lobbyists to undermine progress at every turn. This is not a small, marginal group of holdouts who are leaving the Democratic party. It's easy to make Joe Manchin and Kyrsten Sinema out as villains, but we're talking about almost a fifth of Senate Democrats. Beyond these two senators, this group has included:

- **Senator Jon Tester of Montana**, a state that already has supported a minimum wage above $10, and no subminimum wage for tipped workers.
- **Senators Chris Coons and Tom Carper of Delaware**, two of President Biden's closest allies in the Senate.
- **Senators Jeanne Shaheen and Maggie Hassan of New Hampshire**, allies of a New Hampshire restaurateur who also served on the board of the National Restaurant Association.
- **Senator Angus King of Maine**, an independent who says he supports raising the minimum wage to $15 per hour, yet is so against eliminating the tip credit that he was willing to oppose a bill that would accomplish both.

There are hundreds of corporations and business leaders who wage their own individual fights against raising the minimum wage, but the biggest players in this space are the industry associations. As the official political representatives of thousands of businesses, or entire industries, these entities wield enormous amounts of clout and money to influence policy—usually in the wrong direction. It's hard to overstate how much power these deep-pocketed organizations exercise. Their lobbyists aren't just advising a few members of Congress; in some cases, they're literally writing bills themselves. In the minimum-wage fight, two of the country's largest business associations, the Chamber of Commerce and the National Restaurant Association, have fought so hard, so effectively, and for so long against any increases that they can be almost single-handedly blamed for the current state of the federal minimum wage.

National Restaurant Association

As a representative of some of the biggest, most profitable, and often most exploitative businesses in the restaurant industry, the National Restaurant Association, or "the other NRA," has fought for years to keep the tipped minimum wage for restaurant workers as low as possible. While it ostensibly serves the industry as a whole, the majority of both its funding and its leadership come from large chain corporations like Darden (the parent company of Olive Garden), Dine Brands Global (the parent company of IHOP and Applebee's), Denny's, and Disney, and its lobbying efforts reflect their desperate desire to continue paying their employees as little as possible.[4]

Since its inception back in 1919, the NRA has fought against extending wage protections to restaurant workers. It's got an impressive, if morally dubious, track record. It successfully fought for carve-outs for restaurant workers in the original Fair Labor Standards Act (FLSA) in 1938.[5] It fought for the introduction of a tipped minimum wage to the FLSA when the law was updated in 1966. It has successfully battled to freeze the tipped minimum wage since 1991, and just three years ago was able to kill Democrats' attempts to raise both the federal minimum wage and the tipped minimum wage in the 2021 American Rescue Plan.

The NRA and its member corporations are able to win these fights over and over again because they spend so much more on lobbying and campaign contributions than any worker advocacy groups can muster. One could argue that is inevitable given the wealth disparity between the two factions, but recent reporting reveals there is another surprising, and important, reason: the NRA is making restaurant workers pay for lobbying against improving the workers' own wages.

Back in 2007, the NRA bought ServSafe, an online food safety training program for restaurant workers, and then lobbied many states to make that type of training mandatory for all "food handlers" in restaurants, paid for out of the employees' own pockets. Since 2010, the NRA has taken in more than $25 million in revenue from more than 3.6 million workers who have had to each pay $15 to take the ServSafe course. ServSafe fees go directly into the organization's general funding pool, which in recent years has been skewed more and more toward aggressive lobbying against increasing the tipped minimum wage.

Between 2007 and 2021, the NRA more than doubled its spending on advocacy and lobbying. Over the last decade, it spent $38.4 million on lobbying alone. It also boosted the number of lobbyists on its payroll, many of whom are former government officials who milk their established connections on the Hill to score legislative wins—most notably, the NRA's executive vice president, Sean Kennedy, who served as a senior official in the Obama White House. There's unfortunately nothing illegal about political insiders cashing in on their contacts and influence, but that doesn't make it any less odious.

Points of Contention

You'd be hard-pressed to find many members of the public, or Congress, who believe that the current federal minimum wage is a fair wage. Perhaps there are still a few radical conservative ideologues who believe that we should eliminate a minimum wage entirely, but for the most part, everyone agrees something must be done. Unfortunately, that's about where the agreement ends. As previously demonstrated, there are serious differences not only between the Republican and Democratic parties, but also between members of the same party. The NRA, the Chamber of Commerce, and other lobbying groups have worked hard to confuse and muddy the issue. The big-money interests find as many ways as possible for the lawmakers they support to disagree while sounding somewhat reasonable. As a result, there are now five major points of contention in Congress during minimum-wage negotiations. They are:

- **Amount:** How much should we raise the minimum wage?
- **Phase-in Time:** How long should it take to get there?
- **The National vs. Regional Question:** Should all parts of the country have the same minimum wage?

- **Indexing:** Should the minimum wage automatically increase over time, and if so, how?
- **Tipped Minimum Wage:** Should employers be allowed to count tips toward all or part of their obligation to pay the minimum wage?

How Much Is Enough?

Let's start with the biggest questions: How much should we raise the minimum wage? How much is fair? Initially, the fight for fairness started with a demand to increase the minimum to $10 per hour. Then we had the Fight for $15. Now, progressives are pushing for $17 per hour. To conservative politicians who ignore the inevitable rise of inflation, this proves that the liberals will never be satisfied. People who aren't ideologically and financially committed to paying workers as little as possible, however, recognize that as our economy grows over time, so should our expectations for how workers are paid. Clearly, $10 per hour in 2000 does not buy as much as $10 per hour in 2025. Given changing economic conditions, the demands by the most aggressive supporters of increasing the minimum wage are consistent—wages need to be high enough for workers to pay their bills. If anything, progressives have become less ambitious as time has passed.

The question "How high should the federal minimum wage be?" is the fulcrum around which this issue pivots. Workers want to be paid at least enough to afford all their basic needs. Many businesses pay their workers as little as possible to keep payroll costs down and profits high. One of these two sides is obviously more morally defensible, but morality has little to do with how legislators in Washington make decisions.

There's a real asymmetry between these two sides of the argument. Ultraconservatives, including many sitting members of Congress, argue that there should be no minimum wage at all, that employers should be able to pay whatever people are willing to work for. If someone is willing to work for $1 per hour, they say, then businesses should be allowed to pay them $1 per hour. This position is objectively ridiculous. If the labor market perfectly reflected a balance of power between workers negotiating their wages and businesses paying them, perhaps that might work. However, the massive imbalance of power between employers and employees leaves millions of workers perpetually stuck in a weak and eroding bargaining position, and without wage protections offered by the federal government. On the other hand, even the most ambitious progressives have no interest in raising the minimum wage to an unreasonable level. There are no illusions that raising the minimum wage to such a level would be acceptable for businesses.

Extremes aside, federal legislators fall into three groups on this issue. There is a broad group of those who want $17 (most Democrats). Then there are extremists who do not believe in fair labor standards and who want no minimum-wage increase at all (most Republicans). And then there are those in the middle who want some sort of compromise (a mix of Democrats and Republicans). Who wins this debate is almost certainly going to depend on which party succeeds, and by how much, in the 2024 elections. If Republicans win big, they're probably going to continue to do nothing. If Democrats win big, they're closer to having enough votes to go all-in on a significant minimum-wage increase. Things become more complicated if Democrats win but don't have enough votes to pass a $17-per-hour minimum wage through the Senate. They're going to have to explore a different path forward at that point. If they seek significant bipartisan support, a $10-per-hour minimum-wage bill would likely receive a fair number of Republican votes.

Phase-in Time

The next major point of disagreement between lawmakers is how long it should take to phase in the new minimum wage they agree on. Raising the minimum wage is not bad for businesses, but increasing pay for employees too quickly in a single year could be a harmful financial shock for many. To give the business community time to adjust, nearly every minimum-wage plan has a transition period during which the wage slowly increases each year until it reaches its final amount.

The Raise the Wage Act, the Democratic Party's signature minimum-wage bill, would increase the minimum wage to $17 per hour after five years of gradual increases.[6] It would immediately increase the minimum wage to $9.50 per hour, then $11 after year one, $12.50 after year two, $14 after year three, $15.50 after year four, and $17 after year five. Aside from an initial jump of $2, that's a change of just $1.50 per year.

Raise The Wage Act Phase-In Time	
Immediately	**$9.50**
After the **first year**	**$11.00**
After the **second year**	**$12.50**
After the **third year**	**$14.00**
After the **fourth year**	**$15.50**
After the **fifth year**	**$17.00**

The Raise the Wage Act's authors established a five-year timeline as their sweet spot, but the exact timing is open to debate. There's an argument to be made for quicker increases, given how far the current minimum wage has fallen behind the cost of living, and how much ground low-wage workers have to recover. The longer a new wage floor takes to phase in, the longer it takes for millions of workers to reach a wage they can live on. The quicker the increase, the more disruptive it will likely be for businesses. Most businesses plan some increase to their payroll costs each year, but few have the ability to double the pay for their lowest-paid employees within a year. There's always going to be some friction with increasing the minimum wage—the goal is to minimize that friction while lifting workers up as quickly as possible.

Another important point for legislators to consider is the rising cost of living during the phase-in period when determining their new final number. Consider the Raise the Wage Act. Its new wage might be automatically indexed (we'll cover indexing in just a few pages) after five years, but if a $17 minimum wage is passed in 2025 but isn't fully implemented until 2030, that $17 isn't going to be worth nearly as much as it was in 2025. It might be worth just $16 in inflation-adjusted terms, or less. If the phase-in period were longer—ten years, say—then that $17 might end up being worth less than $15. The longer it takes to reach the targeted wage floor, the weaker that floor will end up being, and a dollar or two of purchasing power is a major issue for low-wage workers. When you only make $35,000 a year (the annual equivalent of working a full-time job at $17 an hour), losing $4,000 makes a real difference.

The National vs. Regional Question

For its entire existence, the federal minimum wage has maintained one consistent level for workers across the entire United States. There have been exceptions for certain types of workers (tipped workers, for example) and some types of industries (agriculture), but the federal government legally requires a universally binding wage floor for workers from sea to shining sea. Cities and states are permitted, and are in many ways expected, to raise their minimum wages higher if they have a higher cost of living, while the federal government sets a baseline for everyone. Some members of Congress argue that a $15 minimum wage is too high, and that any wage that might be appropriate for richer states like New York and California, for example, would be so high in poorer states like Mississippi that it would damage their economies.

There are two competing issues here. First, committing to a regional approach where different states or counties have a different federal minimum wage would inherently create a two-tiered economic system that will likely be gamed by big business and their political allies to pay workers less than what they deserve. History on this issue shows that opponents of a higher federal minimum wage will do whatever it takes to keep wages as low as possible across the country. They know that undermining the universality of the federal minimum wage is an effective way to do exactly that. As soon as you abandon making the minimum wage the same for everyone, you open it up to manipulation. By fighting for wage differences between states and regions, they believe they can sow doubt about the merits of a $15 or $17 wage for everyone, and sneak in lower wages in other states. If a minimum-wage increase is going to happen, they'll do what they can to make sure states like Alabama and Mississippi continue to fall behind states like New York.

We want to reiterate: there is not a single county in the United States where $15 is enough for even a single person without a child to adequately support themselves. No facts support this fanciful concern for poor people in rural communities about their jobs being negatively affected by a $15 minimum wage.

To be sure, there are undeniable differences in the cost of living between different areas of the United States, but, given their track record, state and local governments cannot be trusted to bridge that gap with minimum-wage increases of their own. The standard line of thinking on maintaining one flat federal minimum wage is that while there are major differences in the cost of living across the country, it's up to state and local governments to make further adjustments if they need a higher minimum wage. The federal wage floor should be the baseline for everyone, and places with higher costs of living should implement their own higher minimum wages. This is the model we currently use, and it's been very successful in many states. Legislators in places like California, Massachusetts, and Washington recognized that $7.25 was not enough for workers in their states to get by, so they raised the state wage floor to $15 and more.

This approach has been much less successful in other states. There are twenty states that do not have their own independent minimum wage, but instead use the federal floor of $7.25 an hour.[7] Workers doing the very same jobs in those states as workers in California or Washington can be paid—just on the basis of where they live and work—less than half of what their peers in those two states earn. A significant portion of this difference will be eliminated by raising the federal wage floor, but variations in cost of living will always leave some workers more or less worse off.

The most hard hit are workers in big cities in red states. No matter how high the cost of living in those cities is, and how much the city government wants to raise its minimum wage, in many cases it's not only difficult for cities to raise their minimum wage above what rural workers in those state get; it's actually illegal. Many Republican state legislatures have passed preemption laws that forbid individual cities from instituting a minimum wage above the state minimum wage (which, in many cases, is just the federal minimum wage).

Given Republican obstruction and preemption at the state level, maintaining a flat federal wage floor means that workers in big cities in red states are going to get left behind. A minimum wage that's appropriate for a small rural town is inherently not going to be enough for workers in big cities. Nonetheless, without the federal government mandating a higher wage for those urban workers, it's just not going to happen.

There are many general ways to solve our broken system, but figuring out the specifics is not easy. Do you apply a regional approach to ensure that urban workers in red states aren't underpaid or do you aim for a flat approach to make sure that the gap between rural and urban workers isn't cemented into a government-sanctioned, two-tiered wage system? The progressive community has largely rejected the regional approach, knowing that introducing flexibility to the federal wage floor opens it to being weakened and manipulated by conservative lawmakers in the future. They may be correct—there's certainly a reason that the regional approach is more popular among more conservative legislators. But we've seen the drawbacks of a flat approach over the last few decades and, frankly, should aspire to do better.

Although it is perceived to be politically infeasible today, the best approach, policy-wise, may be for the United States to imitate the Australian model. Australia has one of the world's strongest minimum wages. In 2023, its minimum wage was 23.23 Australian dollars per hour, the equivalent of USD$15.63

per hour.[8] But the *way* that Australia selects its minimum wage is more important than the final dollar figure.

In Australia, the federal government doesn't set an arbitrary number, but rather bases the minimum wage directly on the needs of the country's workers. Every year, an independent panel examines all the economic data, from employment data to economy-wide inflation data to the specific changes in the cost of living for a low-wage worker in Australia—what it costs to afford rent, food, and other expenses—and decides what the country's minimum wage should be.[9]

There's no reason we couldn't do the exact same thing, and at an even more granular level. The federal government has the ability to make the same kinds of calculations for each and every county in the United States. In fact, it's so straightforward that someone has already done it! The MIT Living Wage Calculator, which is publicly available at livingwage .mit.edu, has full cost-of-living calculations for every single state and county in the United States. If inequality researchers at MIT can do it, so can the labor economists in the federal government.

With all this data available at such a micro level, the government has the capability to be much more targeted with its minimum-wage changes. If the cost of living dramatically differs between different areas of the country, then why not have the minimum wage automatically track those differences?

The government could set the minimum wage not at a specific number, but at a specific level. For example, the goal could be that a full-time, forty-hour-a-week job guarantees a person 105 percent of the cost of living. Then, using current economic data, the federal government could ensure that every county in the United States has its own updated minimum wage that tracks how much it costs to live there. For a worker or a business owner, finding out if the local minimum wage has changed could be as simple as looking up their county's data every January 1st on some government website.

This would be much more administratively complex than the current model. It might be easier for businesses to game, or it might be unfeasible for any number of reasons that experts have yet described. But this is an idea that's at least worth exploring. There's no denying the current rigged and failing system does not work. We must start being creative about more appropriate ways to ensure American workers get paid what they need, and what they deserve.

Indexing

The next point of contention in this debate is a relatively mild one. Indexing is the practice of tying the minimum wage to another economic indicator so that the wage automatically adjusts each year as that indicator changes. We could escape the need to rely on Congress to pass a law each time the minimum wage needs to be updated and increased; it would adjust automatically.

There are two competing approaches to this. (Well, perhaps three if you count not indexing at all, but luckily there is near unanimous support for indexing in the political world, even among Republicans.) Almost no one thinks we should not add some form of indexing to the next minimum-wage increase. Congress's inability to pass a raise in fifteen years has made it glaringly obvious that we can't trust legislators to keep the minimum wage up to date. Politics has left worker wages to stagnate, so it makes sense to take politics out of this equation.

Many serious proposals take the indexing approach of tying the minimum wage to two indicators, or "pegs": the cost of living and the median wage. Tying the wage floor to the cost of living is relatively straightforward. Every year we take the change in the Consumer Price Index—the most generally accepted measure of the rise in costs of goods and services that the average American consumer purchases—and increase the minimum wage by that exact same percentage. When inflation is high, the minimum wage increases more quickly. When it's low, the minimum wage increases more slowly.

What Makes Up the Consumer Price Index?

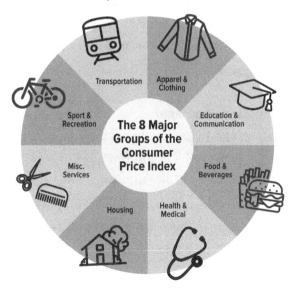

We should note here that describing how the minimum wage would "increase" isn't completely accurate. If applied correctly, indexing the wage floor to inflation would keep it the same, every year, relative to the rest of the economy. The number might change, but a minimum-wage worker's purchasing power would remain the same. This stands in stark contrast to today's system, where the number might stay the same, but as workers face changes in the economy (and as costs increase), their purchasing power erodes with each passing day.

This is an effective model because it hinges on the one thing that is most important to low-wage workers: their true cost of living. They have virtually no wiggle room when it comes to budgeting, so matching pay increases with increases to their expenses allows them to afford their living costs. We know this works: thirteen states and Washington, DC, tie their minimum wages to inflation (although Minnesota and Vermont cap their adjustments at 2.5 percent and 5 percent, respectively), giving millions of low-wage workers in those states a much-needed lifeline as the cost of living skyrocketed in 2021 and 2022.[10]

The second indexing approach, the one used by Senator Bernie Sanders and Representative Bobby Scott in their Raise the Wage Act, is to tie the minimum wage to increases in the median worker's wage.[11] Their bill would raise the minimum wage to $17 per hour and then raise it every year thereafter based on the change in the exact middle point of the wage distribution in America—or, put another way, the point at which exactly half of the country would earn more than that person

States that have tied their minimum wage to inflation

SOURCE: Economic Policy Institute, *Minimum Wage Tracker* https://www.epi.org/miniumum-wage-tracker/

and half would earn less. In the second quarter of 2023, the median worker's wage was $57,200, or about 5.7 percent higher than Q2 2022.[12] For the purposes of indexing, that first number doesn't matter, but the second one does. If the minimum wage had been indexed to the median wage that year, it also would have increased by 5.7 percent (higher than if it were indexed to inflation, which rose by just 4.0 percent).

This approach has the advantage of giving low-wage workers potentially more gains than simply tying the wage to inflation. Using this model, minimum-wage workers wouldn't just keep up with inflation, they could potentially outpace it if median worker pay increases by a higher percentage than the cost of living. It wouldn't just ensure that low-wage workers could maintain their standard of living, it would allow them to increase it as the rest of American workers increased theirs.

This approach has benefits as well as drawbacks for

workers. Median wages normally increase by more than the rate of inflation, but not always. From 2012 to 2021, median wages rose by more than the cost of living every single year. During the stretch of high inflation the United States saw from 2021 to 2022, however, inflation far outpaced median wage growth.[13] Tying the fortunes of minimum-wage workers to that of the rest of American workers might be a good idea most of the time, but during the intervals when the average American worker is falling behind, low-wage workers will lose as well.

Either approach helps low-wage workers, and there are sane arguments for each. The important thing is that the minimum wage is indexed to *something that helps hardworking minimum-wage workers truly afford to pay their bills.* Whatever

A Long-Term View of Wages in America

Average Hourly Earnings Adjusted for Inflation

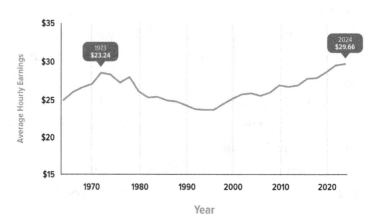

SOURCE: EFRED database, pulled from the Bureau of Labor Statistics' Current Employment Statistics (CES); https://fred.stlouisfed.org/series/AHETPI

minimum-wage bill passes Congress will almost certainly include indexing. Even the painfully inadequate $10 bill introduced by Republican senators Mitt Romney and Tom Cotton in 2021 indexed the new federal wage floor to inflation.[14]

It's a political no-brainer. Aside from the obvious policy benefits, politicians have their own vested interest in making sure this is not a point of discussion in the annual legislative circus. Some lawmakers, focusing on control, want to decide everything the government does, but the political calculus is different for others. For Democrats who care about low-wage workers, indexing the minimum wage is a clear policy win that avoids the historical legislative deadlock that they have been unable to break. For Democrats who care more about their corporate donors than workers, indexing the minimum wage avoids the sensitive topic that creates conflict between two different groups they have to appease, and ensures they don't have to annually vote against the interests of their donors in the future. For Republicans, indexing the minimum wage takes a winning issue away from Democrats at election time—even if some Democrats refuse to take full advantage of it.

GOP Alternatives

Six Republican senators, led by Mitt Romney and Tom Cotton, introduced the Higher Wages for American Workers Act in September 2023.[15] This bill, an echo of a similar bill introduced by Romney and Cotton in 2021, would gradually raise the federal minimum wage to $11 an hour while mandating all employers use E-Verify, a government system that checks whether a worker is authorized to work in the United States and blocks employers from hiring illegal immigrants.

This proposal is a terrible idea on all fronts. The E-Verify system has long been a symbolic weapon for anti-immigration conservatives to brandish. In reality, it just doesn't work. It's a piece of red meat to throw to the more anti-immigrant voters of the Republican Party's base, and expanding E-Verify would be more of a bureaucratic nightmare for immigrant workers and businesses that employ them.

For a group that claims to hate government bureaucracy so much, it's strange to see Republicans try to add a new layer of bureaucracy into every employment interaction in America. It adds enormous amounts of red tape and opens the way for the misclassification of immigrant workers who *are* legally permitted to work in the United States. A report by the Government Accountability Office released in 2010—when only three hundred thousand employers were using the system— found eighty thousand workers were denied even though they had a legal right to work.[16] To make matters worse, there's no particularly effective system to correct misclassification errors. It requires sending in evidence to multiple different departments of the Social Security Administration, a process that can take months. SSA estimates that universal mandatory E-Verify would result in 3.6 million workers annually having to go to field offices and deal with corrections if they wanted to keep their jobs. Who is going to pay for that administrative work?

More importantly, this system fails at the one thing it's designed to do. A study commissioned by the government found that E-Verify failed to catch 54 percent of people who *weren't* eligible to work. For all the costs and complexity that the system would cause workers and business owners, half the time it doesn't even flag the illegal workers it's supposed to identify. Additionally, the federal government's system has been notoriously poor at protecting workers' Social Security numbers and other identifying information from hackers. If we combine these considerations with the fact that it's costly for employers, it's clear that there's basically no upside here—and that is before even considering the obviously anti-immigrant angle.

The wage target of the Higher Wages for American Workers Act is, somehow, even more laughable. Eleven dollars per hour would not be a significant win for workers, it would be an insult. The minimum wage should already be at least $11 per hour. It should have been $11 an hour ten years ago, not five years from now.

With a four-year phase-in period, if the bill were passed in 2025, the minimum wage would reach $11 per hour in 2029, twenty years after the minimum wage was last raised. If the minimum wage had simply been adjusted for inflation since it was last raised to $7.25 per hour, it would already be worth nearly $10.50 in 2024. Using even the most conservative inflation projections of just 2 percent each year, an $11 minimum wage in 2029 will still be worth *less* than what $7.25 per hour was worth in 2009. Romney and Cotton's proposal might sound like progress, but workers will still end up worse off than they were twenty years ago. It's like walking slowly in the wrong direction on a moving sidewalk in an airport—you might feel like you're going somewhere, but you end up behind where you started.

This isn't an oversight on the part of supporters of Romney/Cotton's plan. It's the goal. The dismal state of the current federal minimum wage is pushing things to a breaking point and contributing to an enormous amount of grassroots pressure on politicians to raise the minimum wage. With proposals like $15 and $20 per hour gaining ground, and growing demands to eliminate the tipped subminimum wage entirely, the Republicans we identified earlier are betting that a smaller increase would release some of that pressure while adding no real burden onto the many corporations that are, for the most part, already paying most of their workers at least $10 or $11 per hour. And they're probably right. Banking on establishment Democrats' disorganization and desperation to "make a deal" while appearing bipartisan is often a decent bet. There's a chance that the more moderate members of the Democratic Party would be happy to partner with the Republicans and pretend like the minimum wage has been fixed, even if $11 per hour is still entirely inadequate for most working persons to live on.

It is a clever, if deeply cynical, political move. Worst case, this bill goes nowhere and undercuts the Democratic Party's monopoly on an enormously popular issue. The fact that the bill's existence means this book, and any other coverage of the minimum wage, includes a "Republican proposal" section instantly adds shades of gray to what has otherwise been a clear black-and-white dichotomy between the two parties.

Best case for the Republicans, they pass the bill and

undermine virtually all momentum to raise the federal minimum wage to a fair level, while locking in an inadequate minimum wage for another fifteen to twenty years. As a bonus, they get to include some anti-immigrant policies and appease their anti-immigrant base, reinforcing in the minds of voters and the political media the false notion that immigrants and "real" Americans compete in a zero-sum game for better-paying jobs.

The truth is that working people don't need protection from undocumented people "taking jobs," they need protection from employers who want to pay as little as humanly possible and not have to care about whether their employees can pay their bills. One clear advantage for businesses who hire undocumented workers is that they know those workers have no power to fight back for better wages or working conditions. The Romney-Cotton bill would put all the onus on the workers instead of the problem employers, and tacitly acknowledges that for working Americans to do better, undocumented immigrants have to suffer.

The Human Cost of Low Pay

The fight over wage laws in America isn't just a fight over how much workers should be paid; it's also a battle over who counts as a worker. Workers aren't always given the respect they deserve in this country, but there's at least a consensus, both culturally and legally, about how they should be treated in the workplace, and how little they're allowed to be paid. However, those basic standards don't apply to millions of workers in America who, by the nature of who they are or what they do for work, are defined as different from others and therefore less worthy of protection and fair pay.

You won't find this in any economics textbooks, but throughout American history there's been a consistent rule that if a group is seen as "less than," there are probably some laws on the books that make it easier and legally acceptable to exploit them. The history of wage and workplace protection laws in America boils down to the conflict between businesses and workers—those who want few legal limits to their ability to exploit workers and those who want to be protected and paid fairly for their work. The back-and-forth between these two groups is responsible for the current creaky apparatus of labor laws we have today.

Unfortunately, history shows that there are limits to the general workforce's sense of solidarity with marginalized groups. When voters exert pressure on politicians to make improvements to our labor laws, they generally focus on their own well-being and that of the people they see as their peers. They're unlikely to fight to ensure that groups they don't think about, or don't care about, are included. That leaves an opening for businesses and their powerful lobbyists to wield their influence in Washington to preserve exceptions and exclusions that save businesses a lot of money and cost marginalized workers even more.

This leads to significant carve-outs in America's legal structures that exempt whole classes of workers—such as tipped workers, disabled workers, and prisoners—from minimum-wage laws and other legal protections. This structure must change. We cannot continue to leave millions of American workers behind.

Tipped Workers

There are approximately 5.5 million workers in America right now who earn most of their income from tips,[1] with roles ranging from the commonplace, such as restaurant servers, bartenders, and nail technicians, to the more unusual, such as exotic dancers and casino employees. While many tipped workers at high-end restaurants and bars make a very good living, tipped work is overwhelmingly low-wage work.

Tipped workers are almost three times as likely as non-tipped workers to be earning less than $15 an hour, and the poverty rate for tipped workers (13 percent) is more than double that of non-tipped workers (6 percent).[2] Tipped workers are much more reliant on public assistance programs like Medicaid or SNAP, with 46 percent of tipped workers using at least one of those programs, compared with 35.5 percent of non-tipped workers.

This may be the generally accepted status quo, but these consistently elevated levels of poverty are not the natural result of "market forces." There is no reason restaurant workers, for example, should suffer more from food insecurity than workers in any other industry. What these levels of poverty represent is the inevitable outcome of a set of deliberate policy decisions that undermine the ability of tipped workers to provide for themselves and their families.

Under the Fair Labor Standards Act, there is a special exception for tipped workers that allows employers to pay them less than the standard federal minimum wage. Instead of enforcing the floor at $7.25, the federal subminimum tipped wage sits at just $2.13 per hour, or $17.04 for a full eight-hour shift. That is, to put it mildly, inadequate. Even worse, when you consider taxes withheld from wages, many tipped workers really earn virtually nothing—or close to it, receiving biweekly paychecks that are basically pennies. They rely exclusively on tips they may or may not receive, and have to survive on an enormously unreliable source of income.

We talked about tips in the previous chapter on myths. As we explained there, under federal law, an employer can count a worker's tips against the obligation to pay the minimum wage. Again, the employer is only required to pay either $2.13 per hour plus tips *or* the minimum wage of $7.25 per hour, whichever is greater.

Unlike most other jobs that have a standard schedule and a reliable number of hours, where you know exactly how much money you're going to be paid weekly or monthly, tipped compensation is by nature volatile. You often make less money because weekly or seasonal demand falls off. You may not yet qualify for the highest-paying shifts (in most restaurants, for example, you make a fraction of the amount of money working the Tuesday breakfast shift than you do on the Friday-night dinner shift).

The variables are endless, but they add up to the same result: as a tipped worker, you have a significantly reduced ability to plan your personal finances. Tipped workers are at much greater risk of facing a shortfall through no fault of their own. Imagine not being able to afford to pay your rent this month because of a winter ice storm or a particularly rainy summer. It may sound ridiculous, but it's the reality for hundreds of thousands of people in this country.

There are supposed to be safeguards in place to protect workers from this kind of volatility. If a tipped worker doesn't earn enough tips for their total earnings to reach the minimum wage, employers are legally required to make up

Poverty rates of tipped workers, non-tipped workers, and waitstaff/bartenders by state tipped minimum wage level

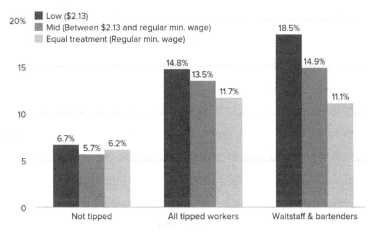

■ Low ($2.13)
■ Mid (Between $2.13 and regular min. wage)
■ Equal treatment (Regular min. wage)

SOURCE: EPI analysis of Current Population Survey Annual Social and Economic Supplement microdata, 2013–2015

the difference. If your tips plus the $2.13 per hour in wages you're already getting paid only adds up to $5 per hour, your employer is supposed to pay you enough to get you to $7.25. However, tips are poorly recorded, wage theft is common, and tipped workers are naturally incentivized not to cause problems with their employers (and you have to suspect that, in the eyes of many restaurant owners, an employee who asks for what they are owed is "causing problems"). With so much of a worker's earnings tied to what shift they're assigned to, asking for money they are owed can easily lead to retaliatory scheduling that hurts their income even more. In the restaurant industry, the squeaky wheel doesn't get the grease—it gets the weekday breakfast shifts.

As a result, people working in restaurants are significantly more likely to face minimum-wage violations than workers in other industries. In fact, 14 percent of tipped workers report making less than the standard minimum wage, even including their tips. More insidiously, forcing workers to rely on tips isn't just a financial problem; it also is associated with an epidemic of sexual harassment within tipped industries. Nowhere is this worse than within the restaurant industry, which has more sexual harassment claims than any other industry in America. Seventy-one percent of restaurant servers are women, and of that group, 90 percent report experiencing some sort of sexual harassment at work.

Because servers are so reliant on tips, a customer in a restaurant has significant power over how much his server is going to earn while she's working his table. This creates an unchecked power dynamic where many customers feel empowered to say or do inappropriate things that they wouldn't do in other establishments (especially when those customers are provided a steady flow of alcohol, which is not uncommon in most restaurants). Servers are then faced with the choice of dealing with the harassment or losing out on that table's tips and not being able to pay their bills. Sometimes, tipped workers don't even have a choice. Because so many restaurants are customer-focused above all else, management will often side with customers over servers. The restaurants that will immediately eject a customer for harassing a server are unfortunately rarer than you might think.

It's also not just customers—many servers are forced to endure harassment or even assault from supervisors as well. Given that servers rely on tips to survive, whoever sets a server's schedule has significant power over their earning potential. Imagine you're a young female server at a family restaurant. One night, your manager corners you in a back room and tries to kiss and grope you. What do you do? Do you quit and hope that you can survive on whatever meager savings you have until you can find a new job? Do you report him to the restaurant owner, knowing full well that the odds of the manager being fired are extremely slim, and that in retaliation, he could start scheduling you for weekday morning shifts instead of weekend night shifts, cutting your tipped income in half? Or do you just grit your teeth and navigate through it, hoping that he won't try to assault you again? It's easy to say that you wouldn't tolerate harassment or assault—until your livelihood depends on it.

This is not a problem that inevitably results from the way restaurants operate. It is a direct outcome of the power dynamics that come from forcing workers to rely on tips. In the seven states where tipped workers earn at least the full minimum wage, women restaurant workers report a rate of sexual harassment half that reported by women restaurant workers in the rest of the country.[3] This suggests that we can fix this problem, or at least greatly mitigate it. We've simply chosen not to.

The Racist History of the Tipped Minimum Wage

If the legal exception to minimum wage is so obviously bad for workers and women, then why do we still have it? For that matter, why did we ever have it in the first place? Like so many other issues in America, the problem stems from a historical legacy of racism and slavery.

Before the Civil War, Americans frowned on the practice of tipping, seeing it as an aristocratic practice that was fundamentally at odds with the American ideal of equality and democracy. Originally imported from European society as a practice that many in the United States considered a shameful imitation of a "master-serf relationship," tipping was opposed so vehemently in parts of the United States that some states even passed anti-tipping laws.[4]

In the wake of the Civil War, however, the practice of tipping grew in popularity as restaurant owners and rail operators discovered they could use it to employ newly freed African Americans without paying them full wages. The deeply seated racial origins of the tipping system weren't so well hidden in those days—it was widely and openly considered a system primarily for African Americans. One journalist in the early twentieth century once wrote, "Negroes take tips, of course, one expects that of them—it is a token of their inferiority. But to give money to a white man was embarrassing to me."[5] This history is why tipping culture is so uniquely American, and why giving a tip in some countries is considered rude.

Fast-forward a few decades to when Congress debated the Fair Labor Standards Act in the late 1930s and, not surprisingly, Southern Democrats refused to accept legislation that would establish a wage floor for African Americans. In a succinct statement of his side's position, Texas representative Martin Dies argue that "you cannot prescribe the same wages for the black man as the white man." To ease these concerns, the bill that Congress eventually passed included exceptions for occupations with a significantly African American labor force, such as agriculture, domestic labor, and restaurant labor. A revision to the bill in 1966 extended some of the bill's protections to service workers, but not all of them; the update introduced the subminimum tipped wage into law, setting a lower base wage for workers who receive tips.[6]

Tipping may not be seen as a racially charged practice nowadays, but its effects continue to disproportionately hurt minority populations. Almost 40 percent of tipped workers are people of color, of whom women of color and immigrants are disproportionately represented.

All tipped workers are vulnerable to swings in income, but Black tipped workers are in a particularly precarious position. Their incomes tend to be lower because they are more likely to work in lower-paying casual restaurants than in fine dining establishments. Owing to racial bias, Black servers are also reliably tipped less than white ones.[7] Black women in particular make almost $5 an hour less than their white male counterparts, and during the COVID-19 pandemic, nine out of ten Black workers relying on tips reported that their tips were reduced by half or more, compared with 78 percent of the tipped workforce overall seeing that kind of reduction in tips.[8] As civil rights advocate Michelle Alexander wrote, "A nation that once enslaved Black people and declared them legally three-fifths of a person now pays many of their descendants less than a third of the minimum wage to which everyone else is entitled."[9]

Stagnation and the Other NRA

Despite its shameful past, the subminimum tipped wage hasn't always been quite as bad as it is now. The tipped minimum wage used to be directly tied to the federal minimum wage, always sitting at or above 50 percent of the standard base wage (not high enough, but a drastic improvement from today's tipped wage, which sits at just 29 percent of an already inadequate $7.25). That changed in 1996, when Congress decided to raise the federal minimum wage from $4.25 to $4.75 without raising the tipped wage along with it.[10] Since then, the minimum wage has been raised four times, but the tipped minimum wage has been locked in amber, remaining at just $2.13 an hour since 1991.

This is an astonishing length of time to leave such a critical piece of our economy unadjusted, and it breaks historical precedent. Between 1966, the year the tipped wage was introduced, and 1991, the longest stretch where it was not raised was nine years. Yet, at this writing, we now live in a world where no American under the age of thirty-three has been alive to witness an increase to the federal tipped wage. This raises an obvious question: Why has raising the tipped wage become so difficult?

Part of the problem is the changing nature of the American political system. As the country has gotten more polarized and the filibuster has ground legislation to a halt in the Senate, any law, not just a wage increase, has become harder to pass. Since the 1990s, the Democratic Party, the only party even pretending to care about the economic interests of working people, has stopped fighting as hard for those same constituents. The move toward a more corporate, more Wall Street–aligned, and less economically progressive Democratic Party may have seemed like the right strategic move in the wake of the Reagan era, but it left millions of Americans without an effective economic champion in Washington.

However, the biggest problem in raising the tipped minimum wage is much more specific to the issue itself. After all, you can't blame thirty years of a stagnant tipped wage on general political dynamics when the standard federal minimum wage was last raised in 2009. There's something uniquely paralyzing about this issue in particular—and that is the enormous power and influence of the restaurant industry in Congress.

The restaurant industry is uniquely positioned to pressure members of Congress simply because of how it is structured. There are restaurants in virtually every community in America, their owners are typically some of the more influential and wealthy members of those communities, and any restaurant shutdown or price increases are noticeable to members of the public. If you're a member of Congress and a group of ten wealthy restaurant owners from your district come to you and insist that a tipped minimum-wage increase is going to force them to shutter their restaurants, lay off a few hundred people, and irritate thousands of their customers (your constituents), you're going to think twice about supporting a wage increase.

There's always been an enormous amount of diffuse pressure on Congress from restaurant owners, but what has changed is how well the industry has organized itself. In American politics money is power, and widespread political support means basically nothing without a well-funded industry lobbying organization. That's exactly what the restaurant industry has got in the National Restaurant Association.

The NRA and its member corporations can win these fights over and over again because they spend an order of magnitude more on lobbying and campaign contributions than any worker group spends. As we detailed in the previous chapter, the NRA's lobbying is prodigious, and it succeeds in part because of the established government connections of its lobbyists.

Industry groups like the NRA claim that they oppose eliminating the subminimum tipped wage not because it will cost restaurant owners money, but because it will be bad for tipped workers themselves and the industry. They argue that it will cause people to tip less and lead to a net *decrease* in earnings by tipped workers, but that's simply not true. We don't have to speculate here—we have seven comprehensive case studies, seven states without a subminimum tipped wage, that prove the contrary.

Workers with Disabilities

When Congress in 1938 passed the Fair Labor Standards Act that created the federal minimum wage, it included an exemption, now called the 14(c) program, for "substandard workers." That exemption was originally included with the hope that it would encourage businesses to hire disabled workers, including injured veterans, and provide them some sort of self-sufficiency and independence.[11] This may have been well intentioned (it certainly was sold as a virtuous measure), but in the decades since, the exemption has been used to take advantage of disabled workers who are less able to advocate for their own rights. It now allows employers to pay disabled workers significantly less than the standard minimum wage, sometimes as little as $1 per hour or less.

The results are unsurprising: a majority of the 122,000 workers with an intellectual or physical disability who are part of this program are paid below $3.50 per hour, less than half the standard federal minimum wage.[12] Only 14 percent make over $7.25 per hour. To make matters worse, instead of integrating these workers into the workforce and allowing them to live independently, as virtually all modern advocates for people with disabilities recommend, the 14(c) program often leads to the establishment of segregated residential workshops where intellectually or developmentally disabled workers perform rote, menial tasks without room for advancement, vocational growth, or the chance to interact with coworkers without disabilities.[13] A 2001 audit by the U.S. Government Accountability Office (GAO) found that only 5 percent of the people at these workshops find outside employment in their community, making it clear that this kind of labor does little to promote the financial independence or personal empowerment of disabled workers.[14] It primarily benefits the businesses getting cheap labor.

There are supposed to be safeguards to this program, but, as you might expect, enforcement is lax. In fact, the

Department of Labor has done such a lousy job enforcing guidelines that in 2023 the U.S. GAO called for significant changes to be made, and a group of U.S. senators and representatives introduced a new bill to eliminate the 14(c) program once and for all.[15]

No one wants a situation where disabled workers are priced out of the workforce. There is real value in finding ways to engage disabled Americans in jobs that provide them a level of financial independence and personal fulfillment. But we can find ways to help disabled Americans be a part of the workforce, such as offering financial incentives and subsidies to employers, without also exploiting them.

Gig Workers

The following is a June 28, 2023, post from the user d_o_cycler on the website Reddit in its r/uberdrivers channel, titled "Officially Done. 7 Years. It's Over":

> I did Uber dang near full-time for 7 years. After three cars and thousands of rides, I'm stepping away. I'll be honest, getting hit hard this last tax season and having to barrow [*sic*] money to pay was a pretty big deciding factor, but moreover, I just have to be honest. This type of gig employment has ruined my health (I have diabetes now, didn't when I started), not added much to my bank account and really just left me feeling like I exist on the fringes of society. . . . It's just been, well, it's left me with a

really sour taste in my mouth and not much hope going forward. . . . At times I said to myself, "at least you don't have to wake up at 5AM like you used to," or "at least you can dress how you want to." But as the years pressed on, the other voices in my head grew louder. The detracting ones . . . were brutally honest about what I was doing and how ultimately it's a road to destination nowhere, to coin a phrase.[16]

As anyone with a smartphone probably could have guessed, gig work is the fastest growing type of work in the American economy. Thirty-six percent of workers in America identify themselves as independent workers—a dramatic increase from 27 percent in 2016. Of America's 164 million workers, 14 million do only gig work, while another 26 million do some combination of gig and contract, freelance, or temporary work.[17]

As more working Americans fall further behind, with traditional employment offering an increasingly difficult path (or no path at all) out of poverty, millions have turned to gig work as a quick, flexible source of income. When workers struggle to get by, they don't just sit around and starve—they go and get a second, or third, or fourth job. This can be challenging for many obvious reasons, from lack of sleep to distraction at work to finding childcare, but one of the most difficult parts of balancing multiple jobs as a low-wage worker is balancing your schedule. With unpredictable and inconsistent schedules, juggling three 25-hour-a-week jobs can be a logistical nightmare.

It's easy to see the appeal of gig work, then, where workers can pick and choose exactly when and how much they work. Instead of bargaining with some low-level manager for more work hours, they just get in the car when they're free and drive for Uber for a few hours. Instead of balancing three independent schedules, they can work one job and then deliver for DoorDash in their free time. There's more agency, more predictability, and more flexibility. Yet, while the freedom and flexibility offered by gig work provides a lot of value to low-wage workers, it comes at a significant cost.

The Cost of Gig Work

Being a gig worker is expensive. You're required to pay for your own equipment, your operating expenses, your health care, and your Social Security and Medicare taxes, which add up to 15.3 percent, as well as any state or local taxes you might owe. You get no paid sick days, no paid vacation days, no workers' compensation, no unemployment insurance, no disability. You're exempt from federal minimum wage, overtime laws, anti-discrimination laws, sexual harassment protections, and laws that allow for collective bargaining.

In a normal employee-employer relationship, your employer is responsible for providing all the equipment that's necessary to do your job. If you're working in an office, they typically need to provide you with a computer, a desk, a chair, and everything in between. If you're working in a restaurant, they need to provide you with pots, pans, ovens, and cooking ingredients. If you're a lumberjack, they provide the truck, the chainsaw, and the ropes.

If you're an independent contractor, however, you're on the hook for basically everything you need to get the job done. In some cases, that makes sense. If you're hiring a contractor to renovate your kitchen, you don't want to have to worry about buying all the construction tools yourself; you want to simply pay the contractor a set amount of money and have them worry about all of that. But in other cases, especially when the independent contractors aren't acting as established businesses with proper expense tracking, those extra costs can add up, significantly eroding their earnings.

Hidden costs put gig workers, for all the flexibility offered to them, in a much more precarious financial situation than their traditionally employed counterparts. Survey data from the Harvard Kennedy School's Shift Project, which was collected from gig workers and service-sector employees in 2020, shows that gig workers are struggling much more across the board than their non-gig peers who received a W-2:

- About 1 in 7 gig workers (14 percent) earned less than the $7.25 federal minimum wage, compared with zero percent of W-2 service-sector workers.
- More than twice as many gig workers—26 percent compared with 11 percent of standard employees— earned less than $10 an hour.
- More than a quarter of gig workers (29 percent)

earned less than their state's minimum wage, compared with 1 percent of standard service-sector employees.

- 62 percent of gig workers reported losing earnings at least once because of "technical difficulties clocking in or out," compared with 19 percent of W-2 employees.
- The number of gig workers reported using SNAP assistance was double that of W-2 employees using it (30 percent and 15 percent, respectively). One in five gig workers (19 percent) have gone hungry because they couldn't afford to eat.
- Nearly a third of gig workers (31 percent) reported not being able to pay their utility bills, compared with 17 percent of standard employees.
- Over half of gig workers (55 percent) reported that they intended to find a new job, compared with 36 percent of W-2 employees.[18]

Employees vs. Independent Contractors

With independent contractors covering many of their work costs and benefits themselves, businesses can obviously save a lot of money by hiring workers as contractors instead of employing them directly. Some groups estimate that companies save up to 30 percent per worker by avoiding payroll taxes, benefits, and unemployment insurance.[19] This obviously creates a set of incentives that encourage corporations to classify as much of their workforce as possible as independent contractors rather than employees.

However, the IRS has very specific guidelines about what identifies a worker as an employee or an independent contractor. There are three factors at play: behavioral control, financial control, and relationship between the two parties.[20] "Behavioral control" means exactly what the term suggests: the guideline seeks to gauge whether someone is deciding the day-to-day behavior of the worker. Employees are told where, how, and when to do their duties. Employees might be required to use specific tools, or perform a task in a very specific way, while contractors choose the tools they think are most appropriate for the job. Independent workers are typically judged based on the result of a project rather than the method they used to get there. This isn't a clear line, but rather a gradient. The more a worker is told *how* to do a job, the more likely they should be classified as an employee.

The financial control test is largely based on who pays the cost of doing business, and how the employee or contractor gets paid. Is the worker forced to pay for their own tools or equipment, and do they typically pay for expenses like supplies or travel? If so, they are more likely to be an independent contractor.

Finally, the IRS judges the type of relationship between worker and employer. This can cover everything from the language of their contract, to the permanency of their relationship (contractors are typically hired on a per-project basis, while employees are hired for an indefinite period of time), to one of the most important points of contention when it comes to gig work: the "services provided" test, which gauges whether the service provided by a worker to a business is a key activity of that business. If someone is hired to paint a mural in a software company's headquarters, the act of painting that mural is not really a critical part of that company's business, and that painter can be more easily classified as an independent contractor. Conversely, if that same company hires a computer programmer—a type of job much more central to the company's business model—that programmer is more likely to be an employee. It is an imprecise, nuanced system. There's no single factor that allows you to look at someone and conclude that this person is definitely an employee. Everything is weighed in context with everything else. That's what makes gig worker classification so hard.

Gig work clearly aligns with independent contracting in many ways: Gig workers use their own equipment. They can work whenever they choose. There are no long-term contracts or guarantees of employment. On the other hand, many gig work companies do exert some level of behavioral control on their workers, such as requiring that they drive certain types of cars. Even more importantly, these companies are absolutely, completely, unequivocally reliant on the services gig workers provide. The labor provided by Uber drivers or DoorDash delivery people is not just a critical part of those companies' business models—it *is* the business. The company would not exist if it weren't for the gig workers who show up every day.

There's an inherent conflict here, made worse when you consider that most of the things that make gig work align with an independent contractor model are decided by the corporations that employ them, and those same things make gig work harder or more expensive. Is it really fair to judge whether a person is an employee or not based mostly on factors that their employer largely controls? If a company can hire a worker for less money and require them to provide their own equipment, why wouldn't they? McDonald's could start requiring its cooks to bring their own spatulas and pay them a few cents per burger they produce, but that doesn't mean those cooks shouldn't be considered employees.

Uber requires its workers to use their own equipment and gives them flexibility over when they choose to work, but it also exerts a fair amount of control. Alex Rosenblat, research lead at the Data & Society Research Institute, explains that Uber "withholds key information drivers need to make informed decisions about the jobs they take, such as the destination of the passenger; it sets and changes pay rates unilaterally; it sets performance metrics for drivers' behavior; and it deactivates (suspends or fires) drivers who don't perform to the standards it sets."[21]

Uber and other companies are fighting to keep the current independent contractor model, because from a business perspective, it's almost always going to be more profitable to rely on a roster of gig workers than full-time employees. There's little incentive, besides it being the law, to hire low-wage employees when you could call them contractors instead, which is why gig work companies are dedicated to maintaining that classification for their workers.

The Future of Gig Work

As some lawmakers push back against the exploitation of gig workers, there's been a movement to classify all gig workers as employees rather than independent contractors. That would solve some of the problems facing the gig economy, but it would create many more. Formal employment, and all the requirements that come with it, might not be right for many people currently doing gig work—there's real value in some of the flexibility provided to them. The fundamental problem we're facing is that the legal binary distinction between employment and independent contracting is not sufficient to deal with this new form of work. Gig workers need more protections and some guarantee of fair wages, but they should also be able to take advantage of the flexibility that formal employment contracts would make difficult. We need a middle ground that gives gig workers the best of both worlds.

Let's be clear: there is much more we need to do to define a fair middle ground for workers in the new gig world of work. In the wake of legal and political pressure against classifying all their workers as independent contractors, companies like Uber and Lyft have already proposed a new, third category of worker, and a bipartisan group of representatives in the House, including Republican Elise Stefanik and Democrat Henry Cuellar, have done the same.[22] They introduced the Worker Flexibility and Choice Act, which would create a new classification of worker that would make gig workers no longer exempt from discrimination, harassment, and family leave laws. While this would mark partial progress, notably absent is any change to the workers' relationship with wage and overtime laws. Any new classification of workers needs to be focused on the needs and wants of the workers themselves, starting with ensuring that gig workers are entitled to the same wage protections as all other workers.

From Fear to Hope

All human babies are born with the fear of falling. That and the fear of loud noises are the only two fears people are born with.[1] They otherwise have virtually no instinct for self-preservation, no innate awareness that they should avoid dangerous things like fire, pools, chemicals, sharp objects, or clowns. All those fears must be learned, but the fear of falling is not. From our very first breath out of the womb, our own DNA screams at us not to fall.

The human aversion to falling is a primal, powerful force. While we learn to live with that fear as we age, for most of us, it never goes away. Our palms get sweaty when we step too close to the edge of a cliff, or our heart rate spikes when we drive across a tall bridge. These are physiological reactions. We can't just think our way out of them. They are instinctual.

There are not many people who stand on the edge of a cliff every day, but in a sense, the way we have structured our economy guarantees that millions of Americans feel that fear of falling most, if not all, of the time. It's not a physical cliff they face, but an economic one. They know that one day, they are going to take one wrong step and they will fall out of the meager stability they have managed to cobble together into a life of abject poverty and despair.

There's no longer any way to deny that the current structure of the American economy overwhelmingly benefits a small number of people at the top and leaves a much larger group struggling to get by. There are millions of Americans who work full-time jobs and can still barely afford to buy even the most basic necessities for themselves and their families. With a federal minimum wage of just $7.25 per hour, the floor for poverty in America isn't just low, it's subterranean. The United States of America is the richest country in the history of the world, but it also has some of the most abject poverty in the modern developed world.

This is obviously bad for the millions of people living in poverty, but we all pay the price. Such a low and shaky floor, combined with a shamefully inadequate social safety net, means that the people in the middle, and even some people at the top, are unsteady. Even the most comfortable middle-class family is often only one crisis away from financial ruin—and they know it. Millions of workers live in a state of barely suppressed anxiety, trying to live a life of calm with fear bubbling under the surface, fear just as real as if they were standing on the edge of a cliff.

When a round of layoffs during an economic downturn can lead to no work for months, or a single injury or illness can drain your finances, almost no one in America is immune to the whims of fate. Some are certainly better insulated than others, but very few people, even high earners, have a nest egg that could last them multiple years or cover extensive medical bills.

This vulnerability is much, much more real than what some might think. Mark Rank, a professor of social welfare at Washington University in St. Louis, and one of the nation's leading experts on poverty, noted in a 2023 interview with *Newsweek* that "nearly three-quarters of Americans will experience at least one year below the poverty line."[2] It might be comforting to some to imagine that poor Americans are poor because that's just who they are, but the reality of poverty in America is that it's something virtually everyone is vulnerable to.

That looming specter of poverty takes a real psychological toll. Loss aversion is a powerful force—the pain of losing is more than twice as psychologically impactful as the pleasure of winning.[3] This makes sense: if you have savings of $1 million, getting another million dollars will be great, but not really life-changing. Losing the $1 million you had would be life-changing. Fear of loss, just like the literal fear of falling, can change how both the body and mind function. Walking across a balance beam two inches above the ground is easy; almost anyone could do that without a thought in the world. Put that balance beam a thousand feet in the air, and it's a totally different experience. Like the fear of falling decreases our motor skills, the fear of falling into poverty is a chronic stress that grinds away at a person's ability to function normally in society, to be a good parent, a good coworker, a good citizen. With such a low floor for poverty in America, everyone is on edge, and our society is starting to break down as a result. If it feels like in recent years everyone's gotten a little meaner, a little less likely to give grace to others, it's probably because they have. As low-wage workers have either stagnated or fallen further behind on the rapidly rising cost of living, the worst-case scenario for many has gotten even worse. The ensuing stress and fear fray social connections and make people lash out, whether that means flipping you off on the freeway or voting for authoritarian politicians who only offer a message of fear and hate.

Something has to give before society completely breaks down. We can't ensure that everyone in America will be successful their whole lives, but what we can do is raise the floor so that everyone's footing is a little more certain. Raising the wage floor and fortifying it would clearly help those at the bottom, but would will also reduce the stress experienced by those in the middle and at the top. It would make a real difference for someone to know that they could still be on relatively solid footing even if they face some challenges in life—a guarantee that we don't yet have in the United States.

Pay the People!

We are living through a disorienting, divisive time in our country, and Americans are losing confidence in the nation

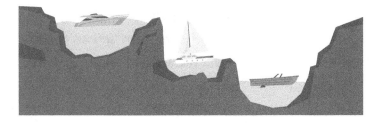

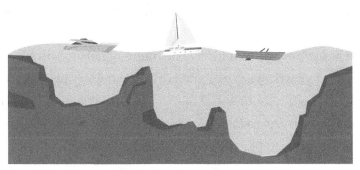

A rising tide lifts all boats—yachts and rowboats!

they love. Today fewer people believe that our country is a land of opportunity where anyone has a fair shot at success. Social mobility was consistent and rising during most of the last century but has fallen dramatically since the 1980s. The current generation of workers understand that their children are likely to be less well off than they are. Students carry more debt into the workplace. Older workers have a harder time paying their medical bills. One of the biggest reasons for the slowdown in social mobility is stagnation in real wages for the middle class and entry-level workers.

Not every problem in America ties to the failure to ensure that companies pay fair wages. We live in an unpredictable and uncertain world. The costs of climate change continue to rise. Leaders of both political parties are perfecting the politics of shame and blame. There are many serious challenges that are out of our reach, but the demand that companies pay fair wages is not one of them.

Once we choose to acknowledge the market's failure to support fair wages and require that businesses assume that function, the benefits will extend far beyond those who get a raise. It will rebalance the obligations of businesses to their low-wage workers and also create more opportunities for everyone to participate fully and fairly in our growing economy and help rebuild our social fabric. When everyone gets a fair share of the proceeds of business, the entire nation can succeed. It's time to pay the people. Let's get to work!

Notes

Introduction

1. Estelle Sommeiller and Mark Price, "The New Gilded Age," Economic Policy Institute, July 19, 2019, https://www.epi.org/publication/the-new-gilded-age-income-inequality-in-the-u-s-by-state-metropolitan-area-and-county/.

2. Howard Schneider, "US Wealth, Income Concentration Resume Upward Climb in Post-Pandemic Era," Reuters, October 9, 2023, https://www.reuters.com/world/us/us-wealth-income-concentration-resume-upward-climb-post-pandemic-era-2023-10-09/.

3. Nick Hanauer, "The Top 1% of Americans Have Taken $50 Trillion From the Bottom 90%—And That's Made the U.S. Less Secure," Time, September 14, 2020, https://time.com/5888024/50-trillion-income-inequality-america/.

4. Josh Bivens and Lawrence Mishel, "Understanding the Historic Divergence Between Productivity and a Typical Worker's Pay," Economic Policy Institute, September 2, 2015, https://www.epi.org/publication/understanding-the-historic-divergence-between-productivity-and-a-typical-workers-pay-why-it-matters-and-why-its-real/.

5. Dr. Amy K. Glasmeier, "Living Wage Calculator," MIT, https://livingwage.mit.edu; Estelle Sommeiller and Mark Price, "The new gilded age," Economic Policy Institute, July 19, 2019, https://www.epi.org/publication/the-new-gilded-age-income-inequality-in-the-u-s-by-state-metropolitan-area-and-county/.

6. "History of Federal Minimum Wage Rates Under the Fair Labor Stan-

dards Act, 1938—2009," US Department of Labor, https://www.dol.gov/agencies/whd/minimum-wage/history/chart.

7. Lauren Cahn, "What the McDonald's Menu Looked Like the Year You Were Born," Taste of Home, June 5, 2024, https://www.tasteofhome.com/article/what-the-mcdonalds-menu-looked-like-the-year-you-were-born/.

8. "Big Mac Index by Country," World Population Review, accessed June 5, 2024, https://worldpopulationreview.com/country-rankings/big-mac-index-by-country.

9. "Inflation Calculator," US Inflation Calculator, https://www.usinflationcalculator.com/.

1. A Livable Wage Is Good for Business

1. U.S. Department of Labor, "History of Federal Minimum Wage Rates Under the Fair Labor Standards Act, 1938–2009," https://www.dol.gov/agencies/whd/minimum-wage/history/chart.

2. Fair Labor Standards Act of 1938," June 25, 1938, available at Fraser, https://fraser.stlouisfed.org/title/fair-labor-standards-act-1938-5567/fulltext.

3. "Inflation Calculator," US Inflation Calculator, https://www.usinflationcalculator.com/.

4. Statista, "Real and Nominal Value of the Federal Minimum Wage in the United States from 1938 to 2023," November 3, 2023, https://www.statista.com/statistics/1065466/real-nominal-value-minimum-wage-us/

5. Marc Davis, "The Spending Habits of Americans," Investopedia, October 17, 2023, https://www.investopedia.com/financial-edge/0512/the-spending-habits-of-americans.aspx.

6. Ivaylo Petev, Luigi Pistaferri, and Itay Saporta Eksten, "Consumption and the Great Recession: An Analysis of Trends, Perceptions, and Distributional Effects," August 2011, https://web.stanford.edu/~pista/cons_recess_August_2011.pdf.

7. Ben Zipperer, "Low-Wage Workforce Tracker," Economic Policy Institute, April 2023, https://economic.github.io/low_wage_workforce.

8. "Family Budget Calculator," Economic Policy Institute, January 2024, https://www.epi.org/resources/budget/.

9. Ben Zipperer and Dave Kamper, "Workers Are 46% More Likely to Make

Below $15 an Hour in States Paying Only the Federal Minimum Wage," Economic Policy Institute, January 13, 2023, https://www.epi.org/blog/workers-are-46-more-likely-to-make-below-15-an-hour-in-states-paying-only-the-federal-minimum-wage/.

10. "Minimum Wage Tracker," Economic Policy Institute, March 1, 2024, https://www.epi.org/minimum-wage-tracker/#/min_wage/.

11. Ben Zipperer, "How Raising the Minimum Wage Ripples Through the Workforce," Washington Center for Equitable Growth, April 28, 2015, https://equitablegrowth.org/raising-minimum-wage-ripples-workforce/.

12. David Cooper, "Raising the Federal Minimum Wage to $15 by 2024 Would Lift Pay for Nearly 40 Million Workers," Economic Policy Institute, February 5, 2019, https://www.epi.org/publication/raising-the-federal-minimum-wage-to-15-by-2024-would-lift-pay-for-nearly-40-million-workers/.

13. Radhakrishnan Gopalan et al., "State Minimum Wages, Employment, and Wage Spillovers: Evidence from Administrative Payroll Data," Journal of Labor Economics 39, no. 3 (July 2021): 673–707.

14. Ben Zipperer, "Low-Wage Workforce Tracker," Economic Policy Institute, April 2023, https://economic.github.io/low_wage_workforce.

15. "Alcohol Consumption by State," Wisevoter, https://wisevoter.com/state-rankings/alcohol-consumption-by-state/.

16. Mike Brown, "Due to Minimum Wage Hike, Some Small Business Owners Will Raise Prices, Rely More on AI, & Possibly Relocate," LendEDU, April 6, 2023, https://lendedu.com/blog/minimum-wage-hike-small-business-impact/.

17. Petev, Pistaferri, and Saporta Eksten, "Consumption and the Great Recession."

18. Franklin Delano Roosevelt, "Statement on N.I.R.A.," June 16, 1933, https://www.presidency.ucsb.edu/documents/statement-nira.

19. "Minimum Wage Tracker," Economic Policy Institute, March 1, 2024, https://www.epi.org/minimum-wage-tracker/#/min_wage/.

20. Julia Rock, "Denny's Shareholders Revolt After Top Exec Concedes $15 Minimum Wage Won't Hurt Business," Newsweek, May 5, 2021, https://www.newsweek.com/dennys-shareholders-revolt-after-ceo-concedes-15-minimum-wage-wont-hurt-business-1588970.

21. Julia Rock and Andrew Perez, "McDonald's, Other CEOs Tell Investors $15 Minimum Wage Won't Hurt Business," *Newsweek*, April 5, 2021, https://www.newsweek.com/mcdonalds-other-ceos-tell-investors-15-minimum-wage-wont-hurt-business-1580978.

22. Cora Lewis, "Businesses Support Raising the Minimum Wage. Why Doesn't The Business Lobby?," Center for Popular Democracy, https://www.populardemocracy.org/news-and-publications/businesses-support-raising-minimum-wage-why-doesn-t-business-lobby.

23. Karl Evers-Hillstrom, "US Chamber Mostly Funded by Small Pool of Big Donors: Study," The Hill, April 26, 2023, https://thehill.com/lobbying/3973039-us-chamber-mostly-funded-by-small-pool-of-big-donors-study/.

2. The State of the Minimum Wage

1. "PwC's Employee Financial Wellness Survey," PwC, January 2023, https://www.pwc.com/us/en/services/consulting/business-transformation/library/employee-financial-wellness-survey.html.

2. Christian Krekel, George Ward, and Jan-Emmanuel De Neve, "Happy Employees and Their Impact on Firm Performance," London School of Economics, July 15, 2019, https://blogs.lse.ac.uk/businessreview/2019/07/15/happy-employees-and-their-impact-on-firm-performance/.

3. Alex Edmans, "The Link Between Job Satisfaction and Firm Value, with Implications for Corporate Social Responsibility," Academy of Management Perspectives 26, no. 4 (November 2012), 1–19, 2012, https://ssrn.com/abstract=2054066.

4. Andrew Van Dam, "The Real Reason Red States Are Hiring So Much Faster than Blue States," Washington Post, May 26, 2023, https://www.washingtonpost.com/business/2023/05/26/hiring-red-blue-states/.

5. Andrew Van Dam, "The Real Reason Red States Are Hiring So Much Faster than Blue States," Washington Post, May 26, 2023, https://www.washingtonpost.com/business/2023/05/26/hiring-red-blue-states/.

6. Joseph Fuller and Manjari Raman, "The High Cost of Neglecting Low-Wage Workers," Harvard Business Review, June 2023, https://hbr.org/2023/05/the-high-cost-of-neglecting-low-wage-workers.

7. Deanna deBara, "Does Pay Matter When It Comes to Employee Reten-

tion?," Lattice, January 12, 2022, https://lattice.com/library/does-pay-matter -when-it-comes-to-employee-retention.

8. Cat Duguay, "Hospitality in the News – Does Increasing Pay Rates Equal Reduced Turnover?," LGC Staffing, April 14, 2022, https://lgcassociates.com /increased-pay-rates-reduced-turnover/#:~:text=Studies%20show%20that %20paying%20employees,impacts%20on%20your%20bottom%20line.

9. Matthew Castillon, "70% of Workers Are Likely to Quit at Current $7.25 Federal Minimum Wage in 'Brutal' Turnover Cycle," CNBC, September 25, 2019, https://www.cnbc.com/2019/09/25/70percent-of-workers-are-likely-to -quit-at-current-federal-minimum-wage.html.

10. Nick Otto, "Avoidable Turnover Costing Employers Big," Employee Benefits News, August 9, 2017, https://www.benefitnews.com/news/avoidable -turnover-costing-employers-big?.

11. Annie Muller, "The Cost of Hiring a New Employee," Investopedia, April 8, 2022, https://www.investopedia.com/financial-edge/0711/the-cost-of -hiring-a-new-employee.aspx.

12. Kate Heinz, "38 Employee Turnover Statistics to Know," Built In, April 17, 2023, https://builtin.com/recruiting/employee-turnover-statistics.

13. Keith Ferrazzi, "Technology Can Save Onboarding from Itself," Harvard Business Review, March 25, 2015, https://hbr.org/2015/03/technology-can -save-onboarding-from-itself.

14. Andrew Jaffee, "The Real Cost of Restaurant Staff Turnover: $146,600 Annually," The Rail, March 17, 2016, https://www.therail.media /stories/2016/3/17/hidden-costs-restaurant-staff-turnover.

15. "Getting the Best on Board," Questionmark, October 5, 2021, https:// www.questionmark.com/resources/reports/getting-the-best-on-board/; Kevin Oakes, "How Long Does It Take to Get Fully Productive?," Training Industry Quarterly, Winter 2012, https://www.nxtbook.com/nxtbooks /trainingindustry/tiq_2012winter/index.php?startid=40#/p/40.

16. Daniel Aduszkiewicz, "How to Structure Onboarding to Speed Time to Productivity," Human Panel, October 25, 2021, https://humanpanel.com /onboarding-and-new-hire-time-to-productivity/.

17. "How Much Will Employee Turnover Cost QSR Franchisees in 2021?," Workpulse, March 30, 2021, https://www.workpulse.com/qsr-employee-turn over-cost-in-2021/.

18. Emma Liam Beckett, "Study: Only 54% of QSR Employees Worked 90 Days before Quitting in 2022," Restaurant Dive, January 20, 2023, https://www.restaurantdive.com/news/most-qsr-employees-worked-90-days-before-quitting-2022/640826/.

19. Sarah Cwiek, "The Middle Class Took Off 100 Years Ago . . . Thanks to Henry Ford?," NPR, January 27, 2014, https://www.npr.org/2014/01/27/267145552/the-middle-class-took-off-100-years-ago-thanks-to-henry-ford.

20. Daniel Gillespie, "No. 1 Reason People Love Their Jobs Is Because of Their Co-workers, Not the Work," SWNS Digital, October 5, 2021, https://swnsdigital.com/us/2021/09/no-1-reason-people-love-their-jobs-is-because-of-their-co-workers-not-the-work/.

21. Daniel Schneider and Kristen Harknett, "Still Unstable: The Persistence of Scheduling Uncertainty During the Pandemic," Shift Project, Harvard Kennedy School, January 2022, https://shift.hks.harvard.edu/wp-content/uploads/2022/01/COVIDUpdate_Brief_Final.pdf.

22. Schneider and Kristen Harknett, "Consequences of Routine Work Schedule Instability for Worker Health and Wellbeing," Shift Project, Harvard Kennedy School, February 2019, https://shift.hks.harvard.edu/files/2019/01/Consequences-of-Routine-Work-Schedule-Instability-for-Worker-Health-and-Wellbeing.pdf.

23. Tracy Colman, "What Does On-Call Mean in Retail?," Top Class Actions, April 23, 2019, https://topclassactions.com/lawsuit-settlements/employment-labor/what-does-on-call-mean-in-retail/.

24. Schneider and Harknett, "Still Unstable."

25. Schneider and Harknett, "Consequences of Routine Work Schedule Instability for Worker Health and Wellbeing."

26. "Census Bureau Releases New Estimates on America's Families and Living Arrangements," United States Census Bureau, November 17, 2022, https://www.census.gov/newsroom/press-releases/2022/americas-families-and-living-arrangements.html#:~:text=Two-thirds%20(67%25)%20of,and%2017%20living%20with%20them.&text=Households%3A,all%20U.S.%20households%20in%202022.

27. "National Single Parent Day: March 21, 2024," United States Census Bureau, March 21, 2024, https://www.census.gov/newsroom/stories/single-parent-day.html.

28. Mahdi Hashemian, Zeynep Ton, and Hazhir Rahmandad, "The Effect of Unstable Schedules on Unit and Employee Productivity," MIT Sloan Research Paper No. 6056-19, September 29, 2021, https://papers.ssrn.com/sol3/papers .cfm?abstract_id=3839673.

29. Saravanan Kesavan et al., "Doing Well by Doing Good: Improving Store Performance with Responsible Scheduling Practices at the Gap, Inc.," Management Science, June 6, 2021, https://ssrn.com/abstract=3731670.

30. Joshua Choper, Daniel Schneider, and Kristen Harknett, "Uncertain Time: Precarious Schedules and Job Turnover in the U.S. Service Sector," Washington Center for Equitable Growth, October 2019, https://equitablegrowth.org/wp-con tent/uploads/2019/10/WP-Choper-Schneider-and-Harknett-Uncertain-Time. pdf.

3. Debunking Myths

1. Adam Uzialko, "How Small Businesses Are Affected by Minimum Wage," Business News Daily, November 20, 2023, https://www.businessnewsdaily .com/8984-increased-minimum-wage.html.

2. Franklin Delano Roosevelt, "Statement on N.I.R.A.," June 16, 1933, https://www.presidency.ucsb.edu/documents/statement-nira.

3. John McDuling, "American Teens Don't Hang Out at Malls Anymore. They Eat at Restaurants," Quartz, APril 11, 2014, https://qz.com/197740 /american-teens-dont-hang-out-at-malls-anymore-they-eat-at-restaurants.

4. Ben Zipperer, "The Impact of the Raise the Wage Act of 2023," Economic Policy Institute, July 25, 2023, https://www.epi.org/publication/rtwa -2023-impact-fact-sheet.

5. Ben Zipperer, "Low-Wage Workforce Tracker," Economic Policy Institute, April 2023, https://economic.github.io/low_wage_workforce.

6. Joseph Fuller and Manjari Raman, "The High Cost of Neglecting Low-Wage Workers," Harvard Business Review, June 2023, https://hbr.org/2023/05 /the-high-cost-of-neglecting-low-wage-workers.

7. Jason Bram, Fatih Karahan, and Brendan Moore, "Minimum Wage Impacts Along the New York–Pennsylvania Border," Federal Reserve Bank of New York, September 25, 2019, https://libertystreeteconomics.newyorkfed.org/2019 /09/minimum-wage-impacts-along-the-new-york-pennsylvania-border/.

8. Claire Kovach and Stephen Herzenberg, "When Low-Wage PA Border County Workers Want a Living Wage Job, What Do They Do? Cross Over into New York or New Jersey," Keystone Research Center, June 15, 2023, https://keystoneresearch.org/research_publication/when-low-wage-pa-border-county-workers-want-a-living-wage-job-what-do-they-do-cross-over-into-new-york-or-new-jersey/.

9. Samuel O'Neal, " 'It's the Right Thing to Do': Meet the Pa. Business Owners Pushing for a Minimum Wage Hike," Pennsylvania Capital-Star, June 25, 2023, https://penncapital-star.com/government-politics/its-the-right-thing-to-do-meet-the-pa-business-owners-pushing-for-a-minimum-wage-hike/.

10. Employment Policies Institute," SourceWatch, https://www.sourcewatch.org/index.php/Employment_Policies_Institute; Michael Saltsman, "Increase in Minimum Wage Kills Jobs," Employment Policies Institute, July 2010, https://epionline.org/oped/0161/.

11. "Illinois," U.S. Bureau of Labor Statistics, 2023, https://www.bls.gov/regions/midwest/illinois.htm.

12. Dom Galeon, "Study Shows That Minimum Wage Hikes Put More Jobs at Risk of Automation," Futurism, August 15, 2017, https://futurism.com/study-shows-that-minimum-wage-hikes-put-more-jobs-at-risk-of-automation.

13. Eric Levitz, "New Study Finds a High Minimum Wage Creates Jobs," Intelligencer, May 13, 2023, https://nymag.com/intelligencer/2023/05/new-study-finds-a-high-minimum-wage-creates-jobs.html?regwall-newsletter-signup=true.

14. Gili Malinsky, "Pay for Low-Wage Workers Grew 'Tremendously Fast' in the Last 3 Years—but Experts Don't Think It'll Last," CNBC, March 30, 2023, https://www.cnbc.com/2023/03/30/low-wage-workers-saw-tremendously-fast-wage-growth-since-2019.html.

15. Mitchell Hartman, "Wage Growth May Be Slowing After Period of Strong Gains," Marketplace, August 28, 2023, https://www.marketplace.org/2023/08/28/wage-growth-slowing-after-months-of-gains/.

16. Lily Jamali, "Wage Increases Haven't Really Boosted Inflation, New Fed Research Says," Marketplace, May 31, 2023, https://www.marketplaceorg/2023/05/31/wage-increases-havent-really-boosted-inflation-new-fed-research-says/.

17. Jasmine Payne-Patterson and Adewale A. Maye, "A History of the Fed-

eral Minimum Wage," Economic Policy Institute, August 31, 2023, https://www.epi.org/blog/a-history-of-the-federal-minimum-wage-85-years-later-the-minimum-wage-is-far-from-equitable/.

18. "Current US Inflation Rates: 2000-2024," U.S. Inflation Calculator, accessed October 2023, https://www.usinflationcalculator.com/inflation/current-inflation-rates/.

19. Jackie Benson, Kevin Cornith, and Kole Nichols, "State Inflation Tracker: November 2022," United States Congress Joint Economic Committee, December 13, 2022, https://www.jec.senate.gov/public/index.cfm/republicans/2022/12/state-inflation-tracker-november-2022.

20. National Restaurant Association and Deloitte, Restaurant Industry Operations Report, 2010, https://s3.amazonaws.com/s3.documentcloud.org/documents/291534/t288-nrarept2010.pdf.

21. Chris Isidore and Vanessa Yurkevich, "September 15, 2023 United Auto Workers Go on Strike," CNN Business, September 16, 2023,https://edition.cnn.com/business/live-news/strike-uaw-stellantis-ford-09-15-23#h_f831655e4e713 2d7d4a0598b6c9fab8c.

22. "The Productivity-Pay Gap," Economic Policy Institute, October 2022, https://www.epi.org/productivity-pay-gap/.

23. Payne-Patterson and Maye, "A History of the Federal Minimum Wage."

24. Aimee Picchi, "Minimum Wage Would Be $26 an Hour If It Had Grown in Line with Productivity," CBS News, September 7, 2021, https://www.cbsnews.com/news/minimum-wage-26-dollars-economy-productivity/.

25. Justin Schweitzer, "Ending the Tipped Minimum Wage Will Reduce Poverty and Inequality," Center for American Progress, March 30, 2021, https://www.americanprogress.org/article/ending-tipped-minimum-wage-will-reduce-poverty-inequality/.

26. Roberto A. Ferman, "Map: Where Americans Are Generous Tippers," The Atlantic, March 21, 2014, https://www.theatlantic.com/business/archive/2014/03/map-where-americans-are-generous-tippers/284567/.

4. The Dumb, the Bad, and the Criminal

1. Brady Meixell and Ross Eisenbrey, "An Epidemic of Wage Theft Is Costing Workers Hundreds of Millions of Dollars a Year," Economic Policy In-

stitute, September 11, 2014, https://www.epi.org/publication/epidemic-wage
-theft-costing-workers-hundreds/.

2. Vanguard Court Watch Interns, "Analysis Raises Important Questions About Corporate Wage Theft vs. Shoplifting," Davis Vanguard, July 26, 2021, https://www.davisvanguard.org/2021/07/analysis-raises-important-questions -about-corporate-wage-theft-v-shoplifting/.

3. Sylvia Allegretto and David Cooper, "Twenty-Three Years and Still Waiting for a Change," Economic Policy Institute, July 10, 2014, https://files.epi .org/2014/EPI-CWED-BP379.pdf.

4. Chris Hacker et al., "Wage Theft Often Goes Unpunished Despite State Systems Meant to Combat It," CBS News, June 30, 2023, https://www.cbsnews .com/news/owed-employers-face-little-accountability-for-wage-theft/.

5. "Work-Life Balance," OECD Better Life Index, accessed September 2023, https://www.oecdbetterlifeindex.org/topics/work-life-balance/.

6. "Overtime," EARN, https://earn.us/issue/overtime/.

7. Heidi Shierholz, "More than Eight Million Workers Will Be Left Behind by the Trump Overtime Proposal," Economic Policy Institute, April 8, 2019, https://www.epi.org/publication/trump-overtime-proposal-april-update/.

8. Marcus Baram, "Will the Biden Administration Deliver on Overtime Pay?," Capital & Main, January 19, 2022, https://capitalandmain.com/will -the-biden-administration-deliver-on-overtime-pay.

9. Lauren Cohen, Umit Gurun, and N. Bugra Ozel, "Too Many Managers: The Strategic Use of Titles to Avoid Overtime Payments," National Bureau of Economic Research, November 2023, https://www.nber.org/papers/w30826.

10. Hugh Baran and Elizabeth Campbell, "Forced Arbitration Helped Employers Who Committed Wage Theft Pocket $9.2 Billion in 2019 from Workers in Low-Paid Jobs," National Employment Law Project, June 7, 2021, https://www.nelp.org/publication/forced-arbitration-cost-workers-in-low -paid-jobs-9-2-billion-in-stolen-wages-in-2019/#.

11. Hacker et al., "Wage Theft Often Goes Unpunished."

12. Hacker et al., "Wage Theft Often Goes Unpunished."

13. Meixell and Eisenbrey, "An Epidemic of Wage Theft Is Costing Workers Hundreds of Millions of Dollars a Year."

14. Judd Legum, "Want to Be a Criminal in America? Stealing Billions Is Your Best Bet to Go Scot-Free," The Guardian, December 7, 2021, https://

www.theguardian.com/commentisfree/2021/dec/07/want-to-be-a-criminal
-in-america-stealing-billions-is-your-best-bet-to-go-scot-free.

15. Hacker et al., "Wage Theft Often Goes Unpunished."

16. Hacker et al., "Wage Theft Often Goes Unpunished."

5. An Added Value

1. Rick Wartzman, *Still Broke: Walmart's Remarkable Transformation and the Limits of Socially Conscious Capitalism* (New York: PublicAffairs, 2022), 215.

2. Julie Murphy and Christopher Shryock, "More Than a Job—A Ladder of Opportunity: Walmart Promotes, on Average, 500 Associates Each Day," Walmart, April 28, 2021, https://corporate.walmart.com/news/2021/04/28 /more-than-a-job-a-ladder-of-opportunity-walmart-promotes-on-average -500-associates-each-day; Jodi Kantor, Karen Weise, and Grace Ashford, "The Amazon That Customers Don't See," *New York Times*, June 15, 2021.

3. Wartzman, *Still Broke*, 214.

4. Ibid., 214.

5. "US Companies and Industry: Largest U.S. Businesses, 2015," InfoPlease, August 5, 2020, https://www.infoplease.com/business/economy/industry /largest-us-businesses-1; "Fortune 500," *Fortune*, 2022, https://fortune.com /ranking/fortune500/2022/.

6. "Fortune 500."

7. Kantor, Weise, and Ashford, "The Amazon That Customers Don't See."

8. Musadiq Budar, "Bezos Vows to Make Amazon 'Earth's Best Employer,' " CBS News, April 16, 2021, https://www.cbsnews.com/news/jeff-bezos-amazon -employee-care/.

9. Aleeya Mayo, "Amazon Delivery Drivers Say There's a 'Giant War' Between Them and the Company as They Struggle to Meet Package Quotas," *Business Insider*, April 5, 2021, https://www.businessinsider.com/amazon -drivers-interview-giant-war-between-them-and-company-packages-2021-7.

10. Jenny Powers, "I'm a UPS Driver. I'm Paid Well and Like the Solitude, but Management Still Makes Me Want to Quit Most Days," *Business Insider*, February 7, 2022, https://www.businessinsider.com/im-a-ups-delivery-driver -what-my-job-is-like-2022-2.

11. Mayo, "Amazon Delivery Drivers Say There's a 'Giant War.' "

12. Ken Klippenstein, "Documents Show Amazon Is Aware Drivers Pee in Bottles and Even Defecate En Route, Despite Company Denial," The Intercept, March 25, 2021, https://theintercept.com/2021/03/25/amazon-drivers-pee -bottles-union/.

13. Mayo, "Amazon Delivery Drivers Say There's a 'Giant War.' "

14. Lauren Kaori Gurley, "Internal Documents Show Amazon's Dystopian System for Tracking Workers Every Minute of Their Shifts," Vice, June 2, 2022, https://www.vice.com/en/article/5dgn73/internal-documents-show-amazons -dystopian-system-for-tracking-workers-every-minute-of-their-shifts.

15. Grace Mayer, "Amazon Warehouse Workers Are Seriously Injured at Twice the Rate of Employees at Similar Warehouses, Study Finds," Business Insider, April 14, 2023, https://www.businessinsider.com/amazon-warehouse -workers-seriously-injured-twice-as-often-study-2023-4.

16. Mark Gruenberg, "Data Shows Amazon Workers Suffer Double the Injuries of Other Warehouse Workers," People's World, November 23, 2022, https://peoplesworld.org/article/data-show-amazon-workers-suffer-double -the-injuries-of-other-warehouse-workers/.

17. Ibid.

18. Landon Mion, "OSHA Fines American Airlines Subsidiary $15k After Worker Gets Sucked into Plane Engine, Dies," Fox Business, June 20, 2022, https://www.foxbusiness.com/economy/osha-fines-american-airlines -subsidiary-15k-after-worker-sucked-plane-engine-dies.

19. "American Airlines Group Revenue 2010-2023," Macrotrends, accessed October 2023, https://www.macrotrends.net/stocks/charts/AAL/american -airlines-group/revenue#.

20. Kris Janisch, "OSHA Fines and Enforcement in 2023," GovDocs, February 23, 2023, https://www.govdocs.com/osha-fines-and-enforcement-in-2023/.

21. "Congressional Proposal Could Mean Massive Increase to Workplace Safety Penalties," Fisher Phillips, September 20, 2021, https://www.fisher phillips.com/en/news-insights/congressional-proposal-could-workplace -safety-penalties.html.

22. Mitchell Clark, "Leaked Documents Show Just How Fast Employees Are Leaving Amazon," The Verge, October 18, 2022, https://www.theverge .com/2022/10/17/23409920/amazon-third-hires-attrition-cost-workforce.

23. Ibid.

24. Jason Del Rey, "Leaked Amazon Memo Warns the Company Is Running Out of People to Hire," Vox, June 17, 2022, https://www.vox.com/recode/23170900/leaked-amazon-memo-warehouses-hiring-shortage.

25. Jodi Kantor, Karen Weise, and Grace Ashford, "The Amazon That Customers Don't See," New York Times, June 15, 2021, https://www.nytimes.com/interactive/2021/06/15/us/amazon-workers.html.

26. Joshua Stowers, "Employee Retention: What Does Your Turnover Rate Tell You?," business.com, November 16, 2023, https://www.business.com/articles/employee-turnover-rate/.

27. "Job Openings and Labor Turnover Survey News Release," U.S. Bureau of Labor Statistics, accessed October 2023, https://www.bls.gov/news.release/jolts.htm.

28. Avery Ellis, "Exclusive: Amazon's Attrition Costs $8 Billion Annually According to Leaked Documents. And It Gets Worse," Engadget, October 18, 2022, https://www.engadget.com/amazon-attrition-leadership-ctsmd-201800110-201800100.html?.

29. Ibid.

30. Ibid.

31. "Amazon.com Net Income (Annual)," YCharts, December 31, 2023, https://ycharts.com/companies/AMZN/net_income_annual.

32. Michael Sainato, "Amazon Could Run Out of Workers in US in Two Years, Internal Memo Suggests," The Guardian, June 22, 2022, https://www.theguardian.com/technology/2022/jun/22/amazon-workers-shortage-leaked-memo-warehouse.

33. Del Rey, "Leaked Amazon Memo Warns the Company Is Running Out of People to Hire."

34. Annie Palmer, "Amazon Hikes Pay for Warehouse and Delivery Workers," CNBC, September 29, 2022, https://www.cnbc.com/2022/09/28/amazon-hikes-pay-for-warehouse-and-delivery-workers.html; Del Rey, "Leaked Amazon Memo Warns the Company Is Running Out of People to Hire."

6. What Is a Job Worth?

1. Laurel Wamsley, "Tyson Foods Fires 7 Plant Managers over Betting Ring on Workers Getting COVID-19," NPR, December 16, 2020, https://www.npr.org/sections/coronavirus-live-updates/2020/12/16/947275866/tyson-foods-fires-7-plant-managers-over-betting-ring-on-workers-getting-covid-19#.

2. Rebecca Wolfe, Kristen Harknett, and Daniel Schneider, "Inequalities at Work and the Toll of COVID-19," Health Affairs, June 4, 2021, https://www.healthaffairs.org/do/10.1377/hpb20210428.863621/.

3. Yea-Hung Chen et al., "Excess Mortality Associated with the COVID-19 Pandemic Among Californians 18–65 Years of Age, by Occupational Sector and Occupation," Institute for Global Health Sciences, January 22, 2021, https://www.medrxiv.org/content/10.1101/2021.01.21.21250266v1.full.pdf.

4. "Families First Coronavirus Response Act: Employee Paid Leave Rights," U.S. Department of Labor, https://www.dol.gov/agencies/whd/pandemic/ffcra-employee-paid-leave.

5. Danica Jefferies, "Who in the U.S. Gets Paid Sick Leave, in Four Charts," NBC News, December 3, 2022, https://www.nbcnews.com/data-graphics/us-gets-paid-sick-leave-four-charts-rcna59801.

6. Abigail Johnson Hess, " 'All Work Produces Value': What Experts Say Eric Adams Gets Wrong About 'Low Skill' Workers," NBC News, January 6, 2022, https://www.cnbc.com/2022/01/06/what-experts-say-eric-adams-gets-wrong-about-low-skilled-workers.html.

7. Annie Lowery, "Low-Skill Workers Aren't a Problem to Be Fixed," The Atlantic, April 23, 2021, https://www.theatlantic.com/ideas/archive/2021/04/theres-no-such-thing-as-a-low-skill-worker/618674/.

8. Matthew Yglesias, "The "Skills Gap" Was a Lie," Vox, January 7, 2019, https://www.vox.com/2019/1/7/18166951/skills-gap-modestino-shoag-ballance.

9. Alicia Sasser Modestino, Daniel Shoag, and Joshua Ballance, "Upskilling: Do Employers Demand Greater Skill When Workers Are Plentiful?," American Economic Association, January 5, 2019, https://www.aeaweb.org/conference/2019/preliminary/1021.

10. Greg Iacurci, "2022 was the 'Real Year of the Great Resignation,' Says

Economist," CNBC, February 1, 2023, https://www.cnbc.com/2023/02/01/why-2022-was-the-real-year-of-the-great-resignation.html.

11. Lauren Kaori Gurley, " 'WE ALL QUIT': How America's Workers Are Taking Back Their Power," Vice, July 23, 2021, https://www.vice.com/en/article/akgy7a/we-all-quit-how-americas-workers-are-taking-back-their-power.

12. Jeanne Meister, "The Great Resignation Becomes the Great ReShuffle: What Employers Can Do To Retain Workers," Forbes, April 19, 2022.

13. "Labor Force Participation Rate," St. Louis Fed, accessed October 2023, https://fred.stlouisfed.org/series/CIVPART.

14. Kim Parker and Julia Menasce Horowitz, "Majority of Workers Who Quit a Job in 2021 Cite Low Pay, No Opportunities for Advancement, Feeling Disrespected," Pew Research Center, March 9, 2022, https://www.pewresearch.org/short-reads/2022/03/09/majority-of-workers-who-quit-a-job-in-2021-cite-low-pay-no-opportunities-for-advancement-feeling-disrespected/.

15. Ken Klippenstein and John Schwarz, "Bank of America Memo, Revealed: 'We Hope' Conditions for American Workers Will Get Worse," The Intercept, July 29, 2022, https://theintercept.com/2022/07/29/bank-of-america-worker-conditions-worse/.

16. Ibid.

17. Aina Marzia, "Students Are Struggling with School Lunch Debt," Prism, April 18, 2023, https://prismreports.org/2023/04/18/students-school-lunch-debt/.

18. Ivana Hrynkiw, " 'I Need Lunch Money,' Alabama School Stamps on Child's Arm," AL.com, June 13, 2016, https://www.al.com/news/birmingham/2016/06/gardendale_elementary_student.html.

19. Krystal FitzSimons, "School Lunch Debt and Lunch Shaming Is a Problem That Needs a National Solution," NBC, October 16, 2019, https://www.nbcnews.com/think/opinion/school-lunch-debt-lunch-shaming-problem-needs-national-solution-ncna1066461.

20. MTV News Staff, "A School District Threatened Families Who Can't Pay Lunch Debt with Family Court and Foster Care," MTV News, July 22, 2019, https://www.mtv.com/news/gav2ux/school-lunch-debt-wyoming-valley-west-pennsylvania.

21. Kate Grumke, "Schools Ended Universal Free Lunch. Now Meal Debt Is Soaring," NPR, May 3, 2023, https://www.npr.org/sections/health

-shots/2023/05/03/1173535647/schools-ended-universal-free-lunch-now-meal
-debt-is-soaring.

7. The Politics of Wages

1. "Two-Thirds of Voters Favor a $15 Federal Minimum Wage, $12 Gets Bipartisan Support," University of Maryland Program for Public Consultation, April 6, 2023, https://publicconsultation.org/uncategorized /two-thirds-of-voters-favor-a-15-federal-minimum-wage-12-gets-bipart isan-support/; Lew Blank, "$7.25 Isn't Cutting It in This Economy. Voters Support Raising the Minimum Wage to $20 Per Hour," Data for Progress, May 24, 2023, https://www.dataforprogress.org/blog/2023/5/24/725-isnt-cut ting-it-in-this-economy-voters-support-raising-the-minimum-wage-to-20 -per-hour.

2. Andrew Prokop, "Study: Politicians Listen to Rich People, Not You," Vox, January 28, 2015, https://www.vox.com/2014/4/18/5624310/martin-gilens -testing-theories-of-american-politics-explained.

3. Taylor Giorno, " 'Midterm Spending Spree': Cost of 2022 Federal Elections Tops $8.9 Billion, a New Midterm Record," OpenSecrets, February 7, 2023, https://www.opensecrets.org/news/2023/02/midterms-spending-spree -cost-of-2022-federal-elections-tops-8-9-billion-a-new-midterm-record/.

4. One Fair Wage and the UC Berkeley Food Labor Research Center, The Other NRA Exposed: The National Restaurant Association's Duplicitous Lobbying, Perpetuation of Race and Gender Inequity, and Support for Insurrectionists, April 2011, https://static1.squarespace.com/stati c/6374f6bf33b7675afa750d48/t/6478bc0cd3de0a74acc619da/1685634061216/ OFW_NRA_Exposed_1.pdf.

5. Ibid.

6. "Raise the Wage Act of 2023," U.S. House of Representatives, 118th Congress, https://democrats-edworkforce.house.gov/imo/media/doc/raise_the_wage _act_bill_text.pdf.

7. "Minimum Wage Chart by State," Employer Pass, January 2, 2024, https://www.employerpass.com/state-minimum-wage-requirements-chart.

8. "What Is the Australian Minimum Wage?," Australia Workers' Union, https://awu.net.au/minimum-wage/.

9. "Annual Wage Reviews," Australia Fair Work Commission, accessed March 11, 2024, https://www.fwc.gov.au/hearings-decisions/major-cases /annual-wage-reviews.

10. Dave Kamper and Sebastian Martinez Hickey, "Tying Minimum-Wage Increases to Inflation, as 13 States Do, Will Lift Up Low-Wage Workers and Their Families Across the Country," Economic Policy Institute, September 6, 2022, https://www.epi.org/blog/tying-minimum-wage-increases-to-inflation-as-12-states-do-will-lift-up-low-wage-workers-and-their-families-across-the -country/.

11. "Raise the Wage Act of 2023."

12. "Usual Weekly Earnings of Wage and Salary Workers," U.S. Bureau of Labor Statistics, accessed October 2023, https://www.bls.gov/news.release /pdf/wkyeng.pdf.

13. Victoria Gregory and Elisabeth Harding, "Nominal Wage Growth at the Individual Level in 2022," Federal Reserve Bank of St. Louis, February 23, 2023, https://www.stlouisfed.org/on-the-economy/2023/feb/nominal-wage -growth-individual-level-2022#.

14. Office of Senator Tom Cotton, "Cotton, Romney Bill to Raise Minimum Wage, Stop Employment of Illegal Immigrants," press release, February 23, 2021, https://www.cotton.senate.gov/news/press-releases/cotton-romney-bill -to-raise-minimum-wage-stop-employment-of-illegal-immigrants.

15. Office of Senator Mitt Romney, "Romney, Cotton, Colleagues Intro-duce Bill to Raise Minimum Wage," press release, September 13, 2023, https:// www.romney.senate.gov/romney-cotton-colleagues-introduce-bill-to-raise -minimum-wage/.

16. U.S. Government Accountability Office, Federal Agencies Have Taken Steps to Improve E-Verify, but Significant Challenges Remain, December 2010, https://www.e-verify.gov/sites/default/files/everify/data/EVerifyGAO Report2010.pdf.

8. The Human Cost of Low Pay

1. Talmon Joseph Smith, "Battle Over Wage Rules for Tipped Workers Is Heating Up," *The New York Times*, October 14, 2023, https://www.nytimes .com/2022/10/13/business/economy/tipped-wage-subminimum.html.

2. "Low-Wage Workforce Tracker," Economic Policy Institute, April 2023, https://economic.github.io/low_wage_workforce; Sylvia Allegretto and David Cooper, "Twenty-Three Years and Still Waiting for a Change," Economic Policy Institute, July 10, 2014, https://files.epi.org/2014/EPI -CWED-BP379.pdf.

3. Debbie Elliott and Emma Bowman, "Tipped Service Workers Are More Vulnerable amid Pandemic Harassment Spike: Study," NPR, December 6, 2020, https://www.npr.org/sections/coronavirus-live-updates/2020/12 /06/943559848/tipped-service-workers-are-more-vulnerable-amid-pan demic-harassment-spike-study.

4. Nina Martyris, "When Tipping Was Considered Deeply Un-American," NPR, November 30, 2015, https://www.npr.org/sections/thesalt/2015/11/30/457 125740/when-tipping-was-considered-deeply-un-american.

5. Ibid.

6. Michelle Alexander, "Tipping Is a Legacy of Slavery," New York Times, February 5, 2021, https://www.nytimes.com/2021/02/05/opinion/minimum -wage-racism.html.

7. Vince Dixon, "The Case Against Tipping in America," Eater, https:// www.eater.com/a/case-against-tipping.

8. One Fair Wage, A Persistent Legacy of Slavery: Ending the Subminimum Wage for Tipped Workers as a Racial Equity Measure, August 2020.

9. Alexander, "Tipping Is a Legacy of Slavery."

10. "History of Federal Minimum Wage Rates Under the Fair Labor Standards Act, 1938–2009," U.S. Department of Labor, accessed September 2023, https://www.dol.gov/agencies/whd/minimum-wage/history/chart.

11. Kate Anderson, "Subminimum Wage: What It Is, Why It's Unjust, and Why It Needs to End," World Institute on Disability, September 28, 2022, https://wid.org/subminimum-wage-what-it-is-why-its-unjust-and-why-it -needs-to-end/.

12. "Subminimum Wage Program: DOL Could Do More to Ensure Timely Oversight," U.S. Government Accountability Office, February 24, 2023, https://www.gao.gov/products/gao-23-105116; Office of Senator Bob Casey, "Casey, Daines, Scott, McMorris Rodgers Announce Bipartisan Bill to Phase Out Subminimum Wage for People with Disabilities," press release, Febru-

ary 27, 2023, https://www.casey.senate.gov/news/releases/casey-daines-scott
-mcmorris-rodgers-announce-bipartisan-bill-to-phase-out-subminimum
-wage-for-people-with-disabilities.

13. "Subminimum Wage Program: DOL Could Do More to Ensure Timely
Oversight," U.S. Government Accountability Office, February 24, 2023,
https://www.gao.gov/products/gao-23-105116.

14. Chabeli Carrazana and Sara Luterman, "Many People with Disabilities
Are Paid Just Pennies. Build Back Better Could Help End That," The 19th,
December 13, 2021, https://19thnews.org/2021/12/subminimum-wage-people
-with-disabilities/.

15. "Subminimum Wage Program"; Office of Senator Bob Casey, "Casey,
Daines, Scott, McMorris Rodgers Announce Bipartisan Bill."

16. d_o_cycler, "Officially Done. 7 Years. It's Over," Reddit, June 28, 2023,
https://www.reddit.com/r/uberdrivers/comments/14llhep/officially_done
_7_years_its_over/.

17. Andre Dua et al., "Freelance, Side Hustles, and Gigs: Many More Americans Have Become Independent Workers," McKinsey & Company, August 23,
2022, https://www.mckinsey.com/featured-insights/sustainable-inclusive
-growth/future-of-america/freelance-side-hustles-and-gigs-many-more
-americans-have-become-independent-workers.

18. Ben Zipperer et al., "National Survey of Gig Workers Paints a Picture of
Poor Working Conditions, Low Pay," Economic Policy Institute, June 1, 2022,
https://www.epi.org/publication/gig-worker-survey/.

19. Nandita Bose, "Rideshare, Retailers Brace for Tough U.S. Independent
Contractor Rule," Reuters, September 27, 2022, https://www.reuters.com
/markets/us/rideshare-retailers-brace-tough-us-independent-contractor
-rule-2022-09-27/.

20. "The IRS Independent Contractor Test Explained," Everee, June 29, 2022,
https://www.everee.com/blog/irs-independent-contractor-test/.

21. A.J. Dellinger, "Uber Says Drivers Aren't Essential to Its Business. But If
They Aren't, Who Is?," Mic, February 21, 2024, https://www.mic.com/impact
/uber-says-drivers-arent-essential-to-its-business-but-if-they-arent-who
-is-18752544.

22. Richard Meneghello and John Polson, "New Congressional Bill Would

Create Hybrid Job Classification for Gig Workers—but Is Already Facing Stiff Opposition," JD Supra, August 2, 2022, https://www.jdsupra.com/legalnews /new-congressional-bill-would-create-9625174/.

9. From Fear to Hope

1. Nadia Kounang, "What Is the Science Behind Fear?," CNN, October 29, 2015, https://edition.cnn.com/2015/10/29/health/science-of-fear/index.html.

2. Giulia Carbonaro, "Poverty Is Killing Nearly 200,000 Americans a Year," Newsweek, June 19, 2023, https://www.newsweek.com/poverty-killing-nearly -200000-americans-year-1806002.

3. "Loss Aversion," BehavioralEconomics.com, accessed September 2023, https://www.behavioraleconomics.com/resources/mini-encyclopedia-of-be /loss-aversion/.

Dedications

From John:

To my wife Lauren, who lifts up our family and laughs at all my jokes. To my sons, Jack and Daniel, you make me proud (almost!) every day. To my parents, whose values and service led the way. And to my grandparents who lived the American dream.

From Morris:

- My wife Barbara who has been with me through everything for a majority of my life.
- My parents, who instilled into me the belief that I could do anything.
- My sons Joshua and Adrian of whom I am so proud.
- My daughter-in-law Donaira who has entered our family bearing so much happiness.
- And my granddaughter Zagora who gives me inspiration to try to provide for her the opportunities, the nation, and the world that my predecessors provided to me.

Acknowledgments

We want to thank the people who made this project possible. Both our team at the Patriotic Millionaires, especially Sam Quigley and René Felt, as well as the dedicated professionals at the New Press: Diane Wachtell, Rachel Vega-DeCesario, Gia Gonzales, and their colleagues. Without these people, this book would not have been possible.

About the Authors

John Driscoll chairs the Waystar Corporation and is senior advisor at Walgreens Boots Alliance. Previously, he was CEO at CareCentrix, president of Castlight, group president at Medco, and SVP at Oxford Health Plans. John also served as a captain in the U.S. Army Reserve and is a longtime board member of the Alliance for Hunger and The Patriotic Millionaires. He lives in Stamford, Connecticut.

Morris Pearl, a former managing director of BlackRock, is board chair of the Patriotic Millionaires. He is the co-author, with Erica Payne, of *Tax the Rich!* and lives in New York City.

The Patriotic Millionaires is a group of hundreds of high-net-worth Americans committed to making all Americans better off by building a more prosperous, stable, and inclusive nation, and ensuring that millionaires, billionaires, and corporations pay their fair share of taxes. It is the co-author (with Morris Pearl and Erica Payne) of *Tax the Rich!*

PUBLISHING IN THE PUBLIC INTEREST

Thank you for reading this book published by The New Press; we hope you enjoyed it. New Press books and authors play a crucial role in sparking conversations about the key political and social issues of our day.

We hope that you will stay in touch with us. Here are a few ways to keep up to date with our books, events, and the issues we cover:

- Sign up at www.thenewpress.com/subscribe to receive updates on New Press authors and issues and to be notified about local events
- www.facebook.com/newpressbooks
- www.twitter.com/thenewpress
- www.instagram.com/thenewpress

Please consider buying New Press books not only for yourself, but also for friends and family and to donate to schools, libraries, community centers, prison libraries, and other organizations involved with the issues our authors write about.

The New Press is a 501(c)(3) nonprofit organization; if you wish to support our work with a tax-deductible gift please visit www.thenewpress.com/donate or use the QR code below.